Successful
Problem Management

MICHAEL SANDERSON

SUCCESSFUL PROBLEM MANAGEMENT

**A WILEY-INTERSCIENCE
PUBLICATION**

JOHN WILEY & SONS
New York • Chichester
Brisbane • Toronto

Library of Congress Cataloging in Publication Data
Sanderson, Michael, 1939-
  Successful problem management.

  "A Wiley-Interscience publication."
  Includes index.
  1.   Problem solving.   2.   Management.   I.   Title.

HD30.29.S26   658.4'03   78-21050
ISBN 0-471-04871-2

PREFACE

I have never failed to be curious as to how people go about solving problems. After spending many years in data processing and management planning, I have come much closer to understanding the vagaries of human thinking, which I had begun to explore as an undergraduate in psychology. Eventually, what most impressed me were some of the delightful ways in which we all conspire to *fail* to solve problems.

At one point in my career I assumed that the best approach was to motivate people to take their difficulties more seriously. I decided that the way to do this was, paradoxically, to make the problems more fun. There followed a flood of cartoon books, posters, and even short satirical plays designed to stimulate new thinking on some of the complexities of management. To a degree this worked. The artwork resulted in lots of fun. However, the outcome was that we now failed to solve our problems with great gusto and enjoyment.

Finally, I realized that I too was failing to solve the problem of why we were not solving our problems—hence my concern with problem definition in this book. My next move was to design a technique that would take some of the heartache out of tackling problems. That is where this book came from. I hope it will help lighten your problem-solving load.

MICHAEL SANDERSON

North Vancouver, B. C., Canada
February 1979

v

CONTENTS

Successful
Problem Management

PART 1

THE STRATEGY

How do you tow an iceberg which is 22 miles by 48 miles? Since 1971 NASA has been keeping watch on an iceberg of these dimensions which has in the meantime drifted 1800 miles. Some thought has been given to towing it to the watershort area of the southern U.S. Here, it is claimed, the water it would produce could satisfy the area's needs for 100 years.

On a smaller scale, a French consulting company called *Cicero* has been looking into the problem for the Saudi Arabian Government. By considering smaller icebergs they have brought the problem a little further ahead, as we shall see later in the book.

But what would you do if you were faced with that problem? Perhaps you would start from somewhere else. Perhaps the real problem is not towing icebergs, but looking for more imaginative solutions to irrigation difficulties. Should you really start by looking for other solutions to the larger problem?

Rushing in and trying to solve a problem as it first appears to us often results in solving the wrong problem. This means that in the interval the real problem has become worse, or the attempt to solve the wrong problem has created a batch of new difficulties.

Solving problems and making decisions or innovations is an activity which requires thoughtful management. Misdirected skills are still misdirected, no matter how skillful. Problem management is necessary to set the stage for flexible and productive work and to guide effort to a fruitful conclusion. Finding out how to tow an iceberg may or may not be an irrelevant over-simplification of a problem. We must think this out before we set to work on icebergs, rather than have it made plain to us afterwards.

The difficulties of problem solving are unfortunately made more difficult by change and uncertainty. Too often the problems we are dealing with are ill-defined and turn out to be more than one problem, or to have multiple parts moving at differing speeds, with all of these cheerfully getting out of control. The entrepreneur is not the only one who moves in a turbulent world. We all experience chaotic conditions at some periods in our lives. That 80% of new businesses fail and that many people only make a mediocre effort at solving their problems points to the real need for skillful problem management.

Today's world is characterized by increasing change and complexity. Situations can change shape rapidly as people take action and as time passes. Complexity and elusiveness conspire to keep solutions one step ahead of us. Our attempts at imaginative solutions are harassed by changes and proliferating details. Depending on your viewpoint, this disorienting turbulence is either a prelude to collapse or the melting-pot of a new renaissance. To avoid the former and accelerate the latter we need capable generalists, people with high-level problem management skills. These are the people now to be found in increasing numbers as entrepreneurs, in interdisciplinary research, and juggling project teams across interdepartmental lines in large corporations. This fast and flexible blending of imaginative, analytical, communication and organizational skills is a skill in itself.

Some kind of overall management of difficult and complex circumstances is clearly called for. We need a technique to

keep us from both dissipating our efforts and failing to respond at an appropriate level. A crucial requirement is a skill
in selecting, organizing, and directing approaches to ever
changing circumstances. The more quickly we can organize
ourselves to deal with fluctuating situations, the more chance
we will have of coming out ahead.

Supporting this problem management skill is the purpose
of the building-block technique of strategy building presented
in this book. It provides pointers, reminders, and a means of
flexibly structuring the many facets that make up problem
solving and decision-making activity. A central concern is the
structuring and use of problem frameworks or strategies.

This is presented in two main parts. In this first part, problem management principles and a methodology are provided.
This is accompanied by some prestructured frameworks at

various levels of detail. In Part II are checklists of questions hierarchically grouped under the principal problem-solving stages. These provide the building blocks. Thus you will find principles of successful problem management, guiding frameworks for specific types of problems, and checklists of questions appropriate to each of the many phases of problem solving and decision making.

In everyday life we may have project management systems to keep projects on course, but we have little other than our thinking skill to keep our thoughts on course. The strategy generator's skeletons and strategies offer us a place to hang our tangential thoughts without constraining our creative impulses. At the same time we are provided with a road map to prevent our losing the thread of our activities as a whole.

The approach is designed to be broad enough for overall guidance of the problem-solving effort, and yet specific enough to be used as a detailed problem-solving tool. As such a tool this technique provides a base which can either stand alone, or be supplemented by creativity techniques, project-planning techniques, decision aids, and other more structured problem-solving methodologies.

Chapter 1

Problem Management Basics

When we are trying to recognize, clarify, and solve a problem, we are attempting to struggle toward something as yet only dimly perceived. We will experience a variety of difficulties. We may have to cope with complexity, vagueness, and confusion. Lack of control and continuous changes of direction may bring frustration. We may see rapid development, high uncertainty, unfamiliarity, or any combination of these. The role of problem management is to allow us to sort out and clarify our difficulties, to stay in control of the situation while we solve the problem, and to make sure we have done it all properly when we have finished.

An important part of the management of a problem is to maintain control from the very start. To make any kind of beginning we need some general guidelines to help us negotiate any hectic events. If the following principles are kept in mind we should be able to make a successful beginning.

FIRST PRINCIPLES

First we must state our objective clearly and unambiguously. This we must do despite our not knowing exactly what form it will take when we attain it. We can say that we want to discover a cure for cancer or a means of conveying eggs safely, without knowing how it will be done.

We should then keep the objective in mind as a guide to all our actions. If we do not know quite where we want to go, how will we tell when we have arrived? Often situations can change alarmingly. Without a clearly conceived goal, or choice of goals, complete disorientation is a real possibility. Even in less chaotic circumstances lack of clarity in objectives can lead to frequent changes of tactics. As a result very little is achieved and the project is effectively out of control.

Another requirement is that we not exhaust our confidence in vain effort by tackling too large a project. We have to adjust our ends to our means. If outsized projects are forced upon us, we must reduce the difficulty stage by stage, rather than attempt everything at once. We do not capture a rhinoceros by trying to lift it in our arms and carry it into a cage. Similarly, when life behaves somewhat like a charging rhinoceros, it is best to show a little circumspection in dealing with it.

Life is short. In order to make the best use of limited time and resources, we must exploit the line of least resistance and choose the path of least expectation. This is not to be confused with avoiding the issue. On the contrary, it is what prevents us from throwing our weight into a worn-out approach to an old problem. This is the key to innovative, appealing courses of action, or to ideas for ways out of sticky situations. We must exercise ingenuity in approaching problems and devising solutions. Ponderous approaches are an unnecessary drain upon the energy of the participants. Our problem-solving activity should have some sparkle.

The approach we take must be flexible enough to adapt to unforeseen circumstances and opportunities. Change is ever present and can often be caused by the activity of trying to solve the problem. Although it is hard to plan for the unforeseeable, a plan which offers alternative objectives will permit good use of new opportunities and/or prevent complete failure. We should never carry a candle into a dark cellar to investigate a strange noise without taking spare matches.

Lastly, if at first you don't succeed, try, try, and try again—but *always* by a different route.

With these principles as a guide we can now look at some of the other aspects of problem management.

The Cyclic Approach

Knowing how to start, and where, can be a problem in itself—as we saw in the iceberg instance. As each problem is different in some way from any other, the first requirement is to be able to select an approach appropriate to our particular situation.

In general, when we solve a problem we proceed in cycles of searching, proposing, and testing. We sense a problem; we form an idea as to what it is; we gather data to test this hypothesis; we decide to attempt to solve the problem as we see it. Then, having established what the problem is, we start another cycle to solve the problem. This problem-solving activity contains a number of phases. We will look at the nature of these phases more closely in Chapter 2.

With most problems we begin with the mini-problem-solving effort of trying to perceive the shape of the difficulty. This is necessary in order to get some idea of where to start, at what level, how vigorously, and using what skills.

Trying to solve a problem as we first perceive it and looking at the solutions we get can lead to new thoughts as to the scope and context of the problem, and may lead to a clearer perception of the real problem. For example, examining a workflow bottleneck between two departments may lead to considering workflow improvements, but it may also lead to looking at other causes, such as interdepartmental rivalry, morale problems, or the overall company policy or style in relation to organization and decision making. An initial run-through helps to pick up on any of these obscured issues.

Depending on the circumstances more or fewer of these cycles of problem-solving activity will be required to give form to, or gain control over the situation.

In some situations actual experimentation may be called for. Here a series of tentative problem *solutions* are tried in real life to get the feel of things.

In the case of designing a new car or developing a sculptural or painting style, this kind of experimentation may be the only way. Obviously this approach must be used with care, as the health and safety of people cannot be jeopardized just to see what happens. Too often this procedure is used not as a means of getting a clear picture of the problem, but as a substitute for solving it. In most cases, such heartache can be avoided by the use of models or games to test solutions or gain a clearer picture of the problem.

In really chaotic situations a number of problem-defining attempts may have to be made in order to bring the situation into focus progressively. If, for example, an organization is faltering, there will probably not be one single cause. It is likely that a complex interplay of economic, organizational, informational, personal, and systemic elements will need to be unravelled. As we often have a particular perception of the causal structure at a particular point in time, and, as situations can change rapidly, a series of different viewpoints may need to be entertained before the true shape of the problem is teased out.

In quite straightforward situations, only one cycle may be required. If the car loses a wheel on the freeway, problem definition is simple. However, in most circumstances it helps to run over the whole cycle at least once to familiarize ourselves with the size and shape of the problem. This means that we would take a look at the problem and make some quick attempts to solve it—without, of course, putting any of these solutions into effect. This is a kind of mental limbering up, which introduces us to the range and difficulty of the problem.

We may well find that during the course of solving a problem we go through recurrent cycles of pulling it all together and pinning down everything, just to get a clear grasp of the problem to that point. Since we can only cope with a certain amount of unstructured information, we will reach a point where we must form some interim synthesis to prevent our being overwhelmed by numerous components.

For example, we may liken the instigation of a particularly complex and stressful management planning project to guerrilla warfare. This metaphor may at least give us some tactical guidelines about which we can construct a course of action to carry us through until we can pin down other phases of the project's design and implementation.

Once this has been done we then elaborate further, develop further ideas, seek more data. These rhythms of simplification—elaboration—simplification seem to occur spontaneously in a person's problem solving. The cycling procedure outlined in this book is intended also to reflect this. Part of the reason for poor problem solving is that we often take the first of these simplification points as our final problem synthesis and do not permit the problem to "mature" by going through further cycles which might lead to more sophisticated solutions. In practice, we may wish to modify the number of cycles in our designed strategy to adapt to the way we are currently experiencing these personal requirements for simplification and elaboration.

Successive approaches can then go into more detail, as familiarity with the problem increases and some conceptions of the required type of solutions begin to take shape. We may, for example, in our initial explorations, find that our problem is not so simple as it first appeared, and that we must use considerable effort to determine exactly what the problem is. Pinpointing social or industrial malaise, or taking a first look at what we want to do in life would be examples. Thus diagnosis, or problem definition, may become a formidable problem in its own right. So we would have to home in on a clear picture of the problem before attempting to plan ways of solving it.

Alternatively, we may find that events are moving so fast and so many things are getting out of control that we have to plan a series of interim solutions in order to stabilize the situation sufficiently to plan a more lasting solution. Local outbreaks of civil disturbance, or guerrilla war, or epidemics could fit here.

If the situation is not amenable to such stabilization, we may have to devote the largest amount of our time to acquiring information and feedback to keep ahead of the game long enough to survive. International politics and, more prosaically, the weather, are examples of this condition.

Many situations break down into series of problems in this way. Part of the skill of problem management is to be able to recognize quickly the type of situation for which we are designing the approach. Later in this book there are "skeletons" of problem-solving approaches for different kinds of difficulty. These are designed to reflect the cyclic approach, which is why there is a repetitive flavor to them.

This cyclic structure can also be seen in a larger framework. As we solve small problems we may uncover or search for other, bigger problems. Having cured a wheat disease, we may then look at increased yield, and then at the problem of transporting larger quantities of grain, and then at international food distribution patterns, and so on. The smaller problems might be seen as cycles contained within an effort to pin down a more nebulous and elusive situation— world hunger. Here the problem grows to encompass a larger area of concern, and operates at a higher level. In negotiating the ever-expanding boundaries of difficulties, careful problem management is required to set limits to a problem's range and to minimize effort and waste. Without care, problems will proliferate faster than we can solve them, while we generate solutions without regard to any larger picture.

Balancing the Approach

So it can be seen that as a situation becomes clearer we may have to modify the approach we are taking, perhaps altering emphases and deployment of effort. Whatever happens, at each point we have to achieve dynamic balances of imagination, judgment, and organization. A well thought-out blend of these is necessary if we are to obtain innovative and productive results. We put together a plan of action or strategy for the purpose of creating a new balance in the world around us. This will be more successful if the strategy to achieve this is itself balanced.

We do not want to spend all our time gathering information and none of it organizing and questioning that information. We do not want to spend all our time in frantic idea generation and assessment, and none of it in the leisurely but vital consideration of ideas simmering on the back burner of our minds. Nor do we want to spend all our time producing fine solutions, only to ruin them with poor implementation, guidance, and follow-through. Provision must be made for all aspects of problem solving to be dynamically balanced against one another. Imagination, organization, and judgment must interweave. Speed and patience, flexibility and control, elaboration and synthesis, planning and tactical redeployment must play their part. Determined, continued effort and a light touch in contemplating larger solutions must balance each other.

In other words, we must be imaginative in thinking out what a problem really involves, but we must be realistic and practical in deciding how it can be tackled. We must have novel and innovative ideas for solutions, but we must be able to turn these into sensible

plans for productive action. Otherwise we may have technicians' solutions to human problems, ponderous bureaucratic solutions to dynamic international difficulties, creative answers to non-problems, imaginative attacks on misconceived situations, and so on. Too much analytic judgment will prevent path-breaking ideas. Too much fantasy will leave us with nothing worthwhile to implement.

To say that a plan or balance has to be dynamic means that we have to set up a course of action which will stay in balance and grow with the world as it fluctuates and presents new instabilities. Rommel's conduct of desert warfare in North Africa in World War II might serve as an example of dynamic planning—a blend of thorough tactical mastery and intuitive flair. Thus, although we may follow a particular problem-solving procedure, external changes may cause us to modify, discard, or improve it as we juggle the balances involved. In the technique presented in this book, these balances are to some extent taken care of at a simple level. However, these must be supplemented by the thoughtfulness of the reader during actual problem solving situations.

Does this make problem management seem as complex as the problems themselves? Without a little care in developing the approach to a problem, this is exactly the position in which we can find ourselves. A hierarchic approach can prevent this.

The Power of Hierarchical Structure

Hierarchic structuring permits us to cope with complexity and build powerful approaches at various levels of abstraction and detail, providing both for flexibility and concentration of effort. We can see the power of the hierarchy in our everyday life as we cope with a surprisingly complex range of matters almost unnoticed. We do this by means of a hierarchy of symbolic concepts. Let us look briefly at what this means.

When we group together a sharp stone, a blade, a pointed stick, and the flattened hand under the concept of "wedge," we find a single name to take care of a wide range of different forms and materials. Also the new concept, "wedge," reveals fresh potential applications. We see possibilities which the mere stick or stone do not point to. Similarly, a brick, a boot, and a fencepost could be subsumed under the concept of "hammer." The concepts "hammer" and "wedge" could be grouped under "tool," and then, with other tools, under "application of force," and so on. This leads to much greater extensions of potential. At each step up in the hierarchy the range of possibilities, the potential for exploration, and the breadth of application are increased.

So when we speak of increasing the range of manufactured goods, preserving the environment, or planning national defense, we are really dealing with incredibly complex structures of concrete and abstract concepts and events. We can use this hierarchic power to control complex situations. Systems analysis as evidenced by the Space Program demonstrates this. But we can also fail to appreciate the complexity of the situation just because it sounds so simple and tidy. Federal and local government often present us with alarming examples of this.

The same qualities can be found in a problem approach as we look at it at different levels. In dealing with problems we can work upwards and downwards along hierarchical paths. Not only can we split a problem into sub-problems, we can split our approach into sections. We can plan our approach by dividing a strategy into smaller pieces. We can break it down into its component groupings and deal with the contents of these groupings separately. This will prevent us from being overwhelmed by the complexity of the task facing us.

For example, we can divide the problem-solving process into planning, diagnosis, idea generation, solution building, and solution assessment. Within each of these we can, as required, make further subdivisions. We will look at this scheme more closely in the following chapters.

At different times, as we deal with a problem we may want to take a broader view or a more specific view. At one time we will be interested in the overall direction and progress of our problem-solving strategy. At another time we will be concerned with specific idea-generating or model-building techniques. With a hierarchic structure we can move around the larger pieces or the smaller pieces, as appropriate.

Using different levels in looking at a problem is particularly useful when dealing with sub-problems. Often when we have gone through a preliminary analysis of a problem, we find that it is in reality several problems overlapping to a greater or lesser extent. In order to be able to deal with these we have to tease out the separate problems and work on them individually. At the same time, however, we have to examine the interactions of these problems and how they form a whole situation.

In such circumstances we need to change levels from time to time, to deal with the coordination and analysis of the problem as a whole, and to deal with each separate sub-problem. To operate solely on one level will certainly lead to inferior results. We may move from a high level to a detailed level or vice versa, depending on whether we are defining a problem or solving it.

For example, we may be in business and have a disturbing feeling that all is not right. We may no longer feel as highly motivated as we did. We may feel that the business is marking time or slipping away from us. In picking out the symptoms of the problem we might start at a detailed level with the immediately apparent difficulties. We might look at staff relationships, the latest productivity figures, or personal health. We may then, on reflection, pick our way into larger problems of the state of the business in relation to the current business and economic context. Or we may wish to reexamine our own life-styles and aspirations, and how our personal goals may be changing. Then when we have pinned down the real problem, we may solve it by reapproaching the situation from a higher level. As though peeling an onion, we remove layer after layer, progressing from high-level objectives and aspirations, down to the details of how to implement our fresh new business scheme.

If we ever have to restructure a project drastically, a hierarchic structure lets us go in from the top down, rather than flounder among a thousand pieces. To regroup, we return to the highest level of the structure—for example, a consideration of the original objectives or the principal standards or values—and work our way back down again, producing a new arrangement of pieces to fit the new situation, even though we may borrow large chunks from our earlier strategy.

If we can borrow pieces from the previous plan, we will be back in action faster. Thus it helps if we do not have to break our earlier strategy up into its smallest components. A child's construction kit would not be popular if it were reduced to undifferentiated blobs of plastic and metal for each model. Such kits are fun precisely because they are already partly organized and ready to be assembled into more complex structures. The strategy-building technique introduced in this book is like a construction kit. It is already partially assembled, but in a way which is still flexible and capable of being built into many different models.

Strategy Building

In the juggling and balancing required of us as problem managers, the more swiftly and unobtrusively we can put together an approach, the more quickly and flexibly we will be able to operate. We want to get into action fast because life demands activity and, often, speed. At the same time we want to act wisely. This requires contemplation. Somehow we must be able to move fast and yet thoughtfully.

One way to do this would be to have a series of ready-made, thoughtful courses of action to select from and match to our situation. In the form of checklisting, this technique has been used in very different ways. It is used to generate novel ideas as in, for example,

Osborn's* checklist of idea-producing suggestions. Idea-generating checklists were subsequently found to be most successful when the number of suggestions on the checklist numbered around seven. Another use of checklists occurs in many systems analysis, work study, or operations research manuals, where step-by-step procedures for effective system design or optimization are listed. This approach prevents our leaving out important activities in the hectic pace of business system design and implementation. A third use of checklists is, of course, the very precise flight deck checklists used by aircrews to be certain that everything in their complex machines is exactly as it should be before the aircraft heads down the runway.

However, in real life we do not often come across situations where we can go by the book in this way. At the same time we cannot plunge into the complexities of today's problems without some kind of guidance. There is not time to reinvent the wheel each morning. Nor are we likely to remember every step or every useful pointer in the problem solving process each time.

What is needed is a tool that will serve all these purposes. It must provide a structured approach to allow us to act quickly, with the benefit of previous tested experience and with both a prompter and a record of our activities. Furthermore, we must have a tool which can match our situation closely enough to give us genuine, practical guidance. This, however, must not be too precisely specified, or we will have to select from many hundreds of predetermined action plans and perhaps still not find one which is quite right. So somehow, before we go into action, we need to have a clear plan of approach, but an approach which can be derived quickly and flexibly.

One way around this difficulty is to start not with complete checklists for each problem situation, but with smaller individual checklists which can be used like building blocks. If each building block offers guidance on a particular aspect of problem solving, it would be possible by following certain assembly guidelines to use these building blocks to produce action plans or strategies of all different shapes and sizes. In this way we have the guidance of past experience built into the building blocks, but without the constraints

*Osborn Alex F, "Applied Imagination," Scribners, New York, Third revised edition, 1963.

on our overall approach that a predesigned checklist would result in. This then allows us to operate in the essentially open-ended problem situations in which we usually find ourselves, which specific predetermined action plans would be unlikely to fit.

Most of the problems which face us in life do not contain a clear goal to work toward. We have to invent the structure of the situation to which we wish to move. There is never just one solution. There is never just one optimal blend. In real life we face difficulties where the only limit to the future alternative states is our blinkered imagination. The strategy-generation technique is intended as a means of dealing with hackwork effectively enough to allow us to incorporate a greater degree of imagination and innovation into our problem solving. This is the basis of the strategy-building technique to be unfolded in Chapter 3.

My technique of strategy building will help to get the reader into action fast to deal with difficulty. Used in the process is a set of 38 strategy elements, akin to groups of checklists. These contain 900 different open-ended questions appropriate to the many different facets of the problem-solving, decision-making, and coping processes. Including those questions which appear in more than one place, this provides over 1200 questions to select from and bring to bear on a problem. A number of ways of using these strategy elements are shown. These range from a simple and speedy use of them as checklists, to complex hierarchic structures.

Except, paradoxically, in the idea-generation sections, there are no dogmatic statements in these strategy elements. Every sentence is a question to be answered. Furthermore, these are open-ended questions. Yes/No answers are not admissible. The questions demand searching and effort to answer them. This does not result in an approach which we blindly *follow*. We remain in control, and guide the course of events with our flexibility, imagination, and judgment. The questions have been selected and structured to support and promote analytic and imaginative questioning in generating novel solutions. They encourage the rigorous questioning of all the ins and outs of a proffered solution. They demand thought from the user, and often self-analysis and assessment, as well as solution analysis.

Important problems which are not seen to be immediately critical—for example, long range strategic planning, clear specification of fundamental objectives and their ramifications, higher-level abstract considerations of policy, morale, motivation, and so on—are in practice often put off because of more pressing concerns. "We've got to tackle that problem some time, but right now we've got to clear up XYZ." To help with these fundamental problems we need a technique that can permit us to come to grips with a problem more quickly and effectively than we presently seem able to, and yet be a methodology so constructed that it allows us to pick it up and drop it as other crises press in on us. The strategy-generating technique, with its self-documenting form, is designed to facilitate this intermittent problem solving. When the technique is used with written answers to questions, it becomes self-documenting. This has a number of advantages:

- If you are interrupted in the course of solving a problem—which is the rule rather than the exception—it permits you to review rapidly and start again where you left off.
- Similarly, when working on three or four problems at a time, it means that the problems are less likely to be confused in your mind, and you can more easily move from one to the other.
- Periodically during the course of problem solving it can be helpful to run back over ideas and information obtained so far to specific questions, and as such can act as a means of getting ideas bubbling again when you seem to be stuck. In favorable circumstances this can result in question answering becoming more fluent, more wide-ranging, and more thoughtful.
- If a problem is dropped or solved, or work is suspended for any reason, the documentation permits later review in some detail, showing where the line of thought may have gone astray or dead-ended. Conversely, bright ideas which were overlooked or ignored, or whose potential was not appreciated, may come to light again.

Questioning is a means of anticipating future events. For example, we can answer the question, "Have I made any false assumptions as to the potential of this solution?" in two ways. One is to implement the solution and experience the answer at first hand. This might have unfortunate results. Alternatively, we can deduce, imagine, or infer the answer—or approximate it—before implementation. This gives us time to adapt our solution if we discover flaws in it.

Through questions can come plans. Through imaginative and

rigorous questioning can come successful courses of action. The strategy-building technique, with its questioning base, can thus be used to support problem management in bringing difficult problems within reach of possible solutions. It can help us to assess solutions carefully so that the difficulties are not regenerated, perpetuated, or made worse by the actions taken to overcome them.

Strategy building is not merely a structure, nor a panacea for resolving difficulties. It is a part of a dynamic process. The problem, the person, the problem-solving effort, and the strategy-building process interact with each other and produce a new situation and foster new skills.

- The strategy-generator question groups eliminate the need to think of a wide range of questions to cover or support problem-solving thinking about a particular area.
- The strategy elements eliminate the need to ponder the range of problem-solving areas or components, and permit a problem-solving plan to be assembled quickly.
- The strategy skeletons, or user-built models, eliminate the need to start from basics every time a problem turns up which bears some resemblance to an earlier problem.
- The mini-strategies of Chapter 4 provide an instant plan of action for some small-scale difficulties.
- The four categories above permit more attention to be paid to the higher levels of problem solving: strategic awareness and overall planning, tactical flexibility, and problem-management activities such as problem state structuring in terms of cycles, balances, hierarchic approaches, and so on.

However, it does *not* detract from the basic skill-through-effort growth potential of the individual's problem-solving power. Rather, by eliminating some of the hackwork, it directs the effort into more demanding areas of problem management, and thus increases the individual's exposure to tantalizing difficulty and facilitates the potential skill development.

At a time when complexity, problems, and change seem to be proliferating faster than our ability to deal with them, some means of solving problems faster and more competently is definitely called for. The strategy-building process is offered as a small step in that direction.

Out of instability and diversity come the boundary conditions which provoke us into seeking new, higher syntheses. We make our way from exploring and fumbling in the dark to theories, solutions, and well-formed procedures. We turn matters for thought into matters of course. With these we again step into the unknown and produce better theories, solutions, and procedures. Out of these new syntheses in turn comes a gradual evolution of boundary condition-handling procedures. The use of these brings us to a further boundary. We seem fated to move ever onwards in a process of reducing the unknown to the known, only to use this knowledge to seek, find, or stumble upon higher degrees of unknown. So we cannot avoid the necessity for imaginative and careful thinking. Nor is there an easy route to good problem management. It is a skill which needs practice and demands effort.

SUMMARY—PROBLEM MANAGEMENT GUIDELINES

Overall:

1. Pin down your objectives clearly.

2. Adjust your ends to your means.

3. Take an unusual approach to make the best use of your resources.

4. Plan with alternate targets.

5. Keep trying—ingeniously.

Approach:

1. Employ cycles of searching, proposing, and testing to home in on the solution.

2. Maintain flexible balances of imagination, judgment, and organization.

3. Take advantage of hierarchic breakdowns and structuring.

Strategy building

A clear plan or strategy will not *solve* the problem, but will help:

1. To prevent the complexity of the situation from distracting us;

2. To reduce the amount of time involved in wondering what to do next;

3. To remind us of things we need to do;

4. To sort out what is going on and to try to perceive some kind of pattern in it;

5. To conceive of a way to deal with this pattern and this situation;

6. To give us the occasional jolt, or injunction to think in a more original manner;

7. To let us consider what will happen if we actually employ our solution, and to see if it is really the best we can do;

8. To extend our ability to synthesize large puzzles.

Chapter 2

Beyond the Checklist

Farming is a tough game at the best of times. So in the early morning when the farmer is trudging through the November mud to feed the pigs, barking dogs may not please him. Particularly displeasing may be the sight of three dogs standing around a dead chicken. "Dangbusted strays!" growls the farmer, as he sees that two dogs are strangers which his own dog is holding at bay. "Chicken-killing dogs can only be cured one way," he thinks, and fetching his shotgun he demonstrates the cure.

Such quick action to take care of a problem and prevent its recurrence is a praiseworthy and sought-after attribute of the first-rate problem solver. However, many of us may occasionally fall into the trap that this farmer fell into.

What trap? The chicken clearly had a broken neck and had not died of old age. So how did its neck get broken? Stray dogs do not stand around a mysteriously deceased chicken and sing Country and Western songs. So what else could have happened? In this instance the chicken did not belong to the farmer at all, but had struggled out of a crate in a passing airplane and broken its neck when it hit the ground. The barking strays—now deceased—were in fact the dogs of the farmer's mother-in-law, who had just arrived for an extended stay. Some obvious solutions to obvious problems certainly raise more difficulties than failing to get out of bed in the morning.

Most of us, when seized with the solution to a problem, can think of twelve good reasons why we should rush into action with it right away. Unfortunately, it only takes *one* good reason why we should *not* move straight away to spoil all those twelve good reasons why we should.

Karl Popper, a noted philosopher of science, has characterized scientific thinking as a series of conjectures and refutations. In other words, he claims, the productive scientist will set up a hypothesis and then attempt to test it to destruction. Trying to find flaws in a solution, rather than looking for more and more reasons why it might be right, will either lead to improvements or detect a disaster before it happens.

To assess a solution rigorously demands more than a nitpicking mentality. It requires the ability to look at things from a variety of viewpoints, and to stand it all on its head to see if it falls apart—in short, imagination. The kind of creative behavior that earlier produced the germ of an idea for our solution is now required to produce the shadow of a doubt that all may not be well.

This kind of niggling should be with us at all stages of the problem-solving process. How do we know we are solving the right problem? How do we know this *is* a problem? How do we know that this is not the worst of seven possible solutions?

It is the role of problem management to ensure that we take account of such things as we solve problems. We must remain aware and flexible. Very often we get carried along, perhaps by habit, perhaps by circumstances, by a particular way of doing things or thinking about events. So it can be of great assistance to have some reminders at hand to keep us out of the traps of habit. If these reminders can provoke in us some imaginative reconsideration and penetrating judgment, so much the better.

If you wonder whether you have the right problem, it might help to consider the following:

1. Are you starting from the right place?

2. Are your facts foggy?

3. Are your interpretations inflexible?

4. Why just look at it from here? It isn't the only viewpoint.

This short list could be used at appropriate points in the course of our problem solving. As we come to grips more seriously with the problem, we may find that it helps to expand our basic list. For example, the farmer with the dogs and chicken might have been helped if the first question were elaborated as below. Any of these questions should have caused him to stumble on a different picture of the problem:

1—1. Why do you see this as a problem?

1—2. Can you be certain that the problem is what it seems to be? Are you sure that *this* is the real problem?

1—3. What unwarranted assumptions are you making? Can you list *all* the assumptions you are making—especially those too obvious to question—and examine each one?

1—4. Why do you think your problem is worth solving? Are your reasons really valid?

1—5. If you have established that a certain factor was the cause of your problem, have you established that other factors involved were *not* also causes?

1—6. Are you looking at information not just for what it shows to be the case, but also for what it shows to be *not* the case?

1—7. Have you considered ramifications outside the immediate problem area?

1—8. Where does this problem fit in the general scheme of things?

If we have a number of these lists for different areas of the problem-solving process, problem management will be simpler. Instead of worrying about the details of problem definition or solution assessment at the time or organizing ourselves to deal with a problem, we can lay out the bare bones of our approach and attach to it checklists like those above.

As mentioned earlier, a problem is much easier to control if approached in a hierarchic manner. In other words, if we rough out a general appraoch—making sure we cover all important areas—we can then deal with the separate areas in a little more detail. As we learn more about the situation we can go into yet more detail, if this is appropriate. This process is made much faster if we have at hand pre-prepared lists of questions for the most frequently encountered areas of problem solving and decision making. Of course, we still have to set up an approach appropriate to our particular problem. However, if we have a hierarchic means of planning it, and some actual pieces to place on our plan, we will be able to get along much faster and operate at a higher level. After that we can get into the details of choosing creativity techniques, project management tools, and so on.

In this way we can move faster to solve more complex problems, knowing that we do not continually have to be remembering and inventing details of procedure. Instead we have only to consider—at the detailed level—how the checklist reminders apply to our particular situation. We can thus devote more of our time to ensuring that the problem is managed and solved to the best of our ability.

This book contains a large number of these checklists. How these can be assembled into problem-solving strategies will be shown in the next chapters.

Before we get into the details of building strategies in this manner, we must look at the background of the problem-solving process. This, in conjunction with the principles expressed in the previous chapter, will help us manage our problem situations more skilfully.

THE PROBLEM-SOLVING PROCESS

The problem-solving process has been divided up in a number of different ways by those investigating our thinking processes. However, most of the breakdowns have much in common and are similar to the one presented here. For our purposes it is convenient to break down problem solving into the following major areas: planning; defining or diagnosing; idea generation; solution building; solution assessment; and approach. Let us look at what these stages involve.

PLANNING

This is where we get organized and decide how we will tackle our difficulty. We have either detected some kind of problem or wish to bring about some new state of affairs. Here problem management begins, and this is the point at which strategy building will take place.

The growth of change and complexity demands a greater amount of conscious planning. If we let three events get out of control, there are 63 possible interrelationships of events which could be set up—excluding the case where there are no effects. If we have five events interacting, there are 1,048,575 possible ways in which they could

affect each other—$2^{n(n-1)}$. This leaves room for a considerable number of unpleasant surprises. It is therefore advisable to try to remain in control of the direction of events. Planning and future anticipation help.

The planning process will encompass and direct all other phases of problem solving. We cannot set up a problem-solving plan merely by lining up a series of techniques, any more than we could harness a zoo to a wagon and expect to make a smooth journey. We must assemble our approach carefully, rather than in a hit-or-miss way.

During the planning phase we establish some objectives for the project, and determine the style of operating which we will use. We will consider why we are doing it, what we hope to achieve, what our action priorities might be, whom we might need to help us, and how the operation might be organized. In the course of this we need to make an initial assessment of the situation. After we have attempted this miniature review, we plan our approach accordingly. During this phase our imagination/judgment/organization blend is weighted in favor of organization.

DIAGNOSING OR DEFINING

Before we start to solve a problem we must have gained a clear idea of what it really is. Trying not to be misled by the appearance of the situation can be difficult, and calls for awareness and imagination. This is a point where we often go astray—usually through impatience. Equally, our habits of thinking can blind us to the real situation. The contexts in which we normally set problems can lead us to misconstrue a situation. Our problem-solving style—or that of the organization for which we work—can obstruct us as much as it may aid us.

We should ask ourselves: What do we think is going on? What are the facts? What do we know? What do we have to find out? When we have what seem to be the facts we must double-check them to see if they are not subject to other interpretations.

If there is, for example, a problem of supplies being late and causing production slowdowns, we should go and see the supplies arriving. Perhaps the supplies are not really arriving late, but being unloaded late. Perhaps the entrance is too small, causing queues. Perhaps unloading machinery is antiquated. Perhaps lateness is not the problem at all. If it is, what does "late" mean? Is it three hours late or three days late? Late for the beginning of the day, or late for process X? A vague problem cannot be solved. Clarify it.

We must also ensure that our growing feeling for what the problem may be does not influence the information we are gathering in a way detrimental to astute analysis. This can often be a difficulty when dealing with personnel problems, especially when we are ourselves quite involved with the situation.

We should also consider whether anyone else has had this problem. If so, what did they do about it, write about it, or say about it, and with what results? What knowledge is already recorded about this kind of problem? Who else has followed this route?

How can we be certain that the problem as we see it really is the problem? Perhaps it is something entirely different? What does the overall situation look like? What else is involved? We may have to use some imagination to make sure we have the real problem.

In an aircraft factory with which I was once involved, looking for stolen components was part of the regular security checking. The problem was apparently how to track down where the parts were being hidden and taken out. One day a car and trailer drove up to the gate. Guards searched the car and trailer thoroughly. Nothing was found and yet something was stolen. How? The trailer itself was made of sheet aluminum and other parts stolen from the factory. Obviously we need to be able to take a flexible interpretation of the definition of a problem.

It can be seen that by the time we have a clear perception of the problem we have already exercised considerable problem-solving skill.

IDEA GENERATION

Now that we have a clear idea of the problem, we will be quite familiar with the whole area. In our explorations, the way things are will have impressed itself upon us. Sometimes this impression prevents us from easily seeing beneath the surface or from seeing other conceivable arrangements of affairs. Original solutions are required. These are hard to entertain unless we somehow set our minds into new channels.

In a library in which I was involved in management planning we found considerable apathy toward management-planning concepts among the staff. One part of the problem was to make these more appealing. This I eventually did by producing a comic book which explained the concepts in concrete and humorous form, relating them to daily operations in the library. In this instance the route to a serious result was by the side-roads of humor.

The concept behind the methodology presented in this book is born of a failure to figure out something in a completely different area. I invented a problem-solving card game based upon rigorously questioning proposed problem solutions. The only problem was that the scoring system had some flaws in it that I was unable to resolve. While pondering this I suddenly had the idea of using the questioning principle in an entirely new form. Hence this book.

So we must think of as many new ideas and reformulations of the problem situation as possible. We twist it around, generate analogies, and look for metaphors. We do *not* stop wild ideas at this point—they may help. If not, they can be pulled out later. We do not let criticism cramp our style, and we try for as many viewpoints as we can.

Gutenberg saw an analogy between a wine-press and a way of

printing. Archimedes saw an analogy between the rising water level in a bathtub and the different densities of metal. Bohr and Wheeler used a surface tension analogy for work on the surface energy of the atomic nucleus before fission. Pilkington's idea for plate-glass was aided by an analogy to grease floating on dishwater.

A more exotic example is to be found in W. J. J. Gordon's book "Synectics,"* in which the problem is to invent a vaporproof closure for space suits. The fantasy used was of two rows of insects, on either side of a gap, holding hands across the gap, and pulling. From this impossible situation came the idea of having a coil spring embedded in the rubber suit material. When the opening is closed, the spring's convolutions overlap and a steel wire is passed down the middle, thus locking them together.

A good example of a highly developed use of analogy is the discipline of bionics. Here we see the search for biological analogies becoming the focus of the exercise. Bionics involves the study of biologi-

*Gordon, W. J. J., "Synectics," Harper Row, New York, 1961.

cal systems in order to develop analogous man-made systems. Looking closely at the forms and functions of plant and animal life can lead us to the discovery of principles that can be used to solve problems in other fields.

Part of the rationale is that nature has successfully adapted to many strange and difficult circumstances. Some of the myriads of incredible designs that have resulted from these adaptations can be adopted or modified, or trigger off other useful ideas.

Study of the beetle's eye has led to the development of a superior ground-speed indicator for aircraft. The dragonfly's hovering characteristics have been investigated to shed light on low-level hovering problems in helicopters. But there are many other possibilities. Nylon closure strips based on the sticking qualities of burrs from plants are an everyday example.

When pursuing our analogies, metaphors, or wild ideas, we do not exert too much pressure for answers, since anxiety can act to keep us frantically thinking in familiar old ruts. However, we still keep it all hovering in our minds, gently coaxing those sparks of ingenuity.

We need to generate a large number of ideas. In any group of ideas the later ones are usually of better quality. First ideas are often rather prosaic and uninspired. So the more ideas the better.

This is all done for the purpose of synthesizing new concepts. Creativity techniques can be incorporated here, but the strategy elements given later, plus an open and motivated mind, are enough for a good start.

SOLUTION BUILDING

A solution starts from an idea which gives it shape and unity. But the idea is only the start. It is more of an abstraction, a skeleton, or framework. Now we must carefully put together all the pieces of the real world situation around our new idea.

We may decide that we can make steel more profitably by computerizing the steel cast analysis, and thus satisfy a wider range of orders from each cast. However, if we do not look closely at all the practical implications of the idea we may lose money rather than make profits.

It is essential to specify how the solution will relate to current objectives or policies, what standards of operation and organization it will aim for, and how its success in achieving these will be measured.

It must be shown how people will fit in, at what points and why, how effort and information will flow, when, how quickly, in what volumes and forms, when and where decisions will be made, why, and by whom.

It must be clear how all the procedures and functions will fit together and balance each other, and how connections with other systems will be made. For example, how will we deal with the telephone system, the government, the purchasing department, our neighbors, the political climate, and so on, as they apply to our situation?

How will our solution react to change, how will it develop, what will it cost, what planning and forecasting will it encompass, how will it cope with problems, and how will it be directed? Where will it all lead? What ramifications are there now and for the future? Can we build some kind of model of the situation to explore and pretest solutions? How will we introduce our solution into the world? How does everything fit together?

For example, in considering a computerized steel cast amalgamation program, many factors need to be considered in addition to the most obvious problem. A steel corporation with a number of plant locations, furnace types, and processing specializations considered a computer system to improve the efficiency of filling steel orders. Several hundred different kinds of steel could be made to order. To avoid making small amounts of an absolutely precise analysis of steel for each customer, the procedure was to lump together orders whose analysis tolerances overlapped, and thus to make one large amount of steel to satisfy several orders. The basic idea was to computerize this process to make it faster and more efficient. Problems arose when building the idea into a solution which could actually be implemented. To *make* the steel was one thing. The subsequent processing of the steel according to the customer's requirements and shipping it to the customer were also important factors. These determined whether or not steel orders could be lumped together and made at a particular location. A special type of treatment might mean shipping an order to a different location. Then increased shipping distances might result in further inconvenience to the customer. The added transportation, handling, and paperwork might exceed the savings made by amalgamating the orders. The complexity of the solution can thus often be much greater than the apparent simplicity of the basic idea for a solution.

We have to make our idea grow into a solution and then see how it will look in real life. We take our ideas and turn them into practical, workable solutions. We want no loose ends. We have to make sure we have covered every contingency—as far as this is sensibly possible. There is a world of difference between a bright idea and an innovative, practial solution—as we see only too often in our daily affairs.

SOLUTION ASSESSMENT

Before we put a solution into effect, we must be sure it is the best one. Preferably we will have thought of more than one solution to the problem, each with its own peculiar advantages. Badly thought-out solutions cause at least as much harm as having done nothing. So we might as well spend the time doing things properly.

Now we look at what is wrong with our solution. Is there anything we feel even slightly uneasy about? What have we overlooked?

Maybe this is not the right answer at all? What will the future of the solution be? Will the pieces always fit so nicely? What could change, and have we allowed for it? What would be a disaster for this solution? Is it flexible enough to cope with the future?

Some of the various techniques that can help us find flaws in our favorite brainchild are: statistical analysis thoughtfully applied; the careful design of tests and experiments; survey; opinion polls; pilot schemes tried out on a small scale; running the solution in parallel with the present situation where possible; simulations; game situations; and cost/benefit analyses.

If our solution has survived so far, perhaps it can be made even better. Now we take its best points and see if they can be improved. We pick its worst points and see if they can be cut out. Can it be extended to solve problems elsewhere? It helps to let the problem rest for a while, so that we can go over it again with a changed perspective. We should keep trying to improve the good and eliminate the bad.

Let us consider two examples of the need for care in solution assessment. Paul Ehrlich in "The Population Bomb"* describes how in 1966 the United States shipped one quarter of her wheat crop, nine million tons, to India. He maintains that as a result of doing so the distribution of people in the country was changed. People moved to the ports to be close to the centers of wheat distribution. Some have claimed that India's own agricultural development was hindered by letting it be thought that the U.S. could continue to supply needs. Here the solution contributes to a continuation of the problem.

A second example of unforeseen consequences of an apparently good solution is the Australian experience with the poisonous giant toads. These were imported to Australia to deal with the beetles which damage sugar cane. However, after the toads had been in Australia for awhile, they started to eat other beetles, and not the ones they were supposed to eat. So the problem persisted. Furthermore, the toads also poisoned the snakes and birds which ate other pests. Thus the solution turned into another problem.

Not only is it necessary to look ahead for possible ill effects of solutions, it is essential that this be done with considerable imagination.

*Ehrlich, Paul R. "The Population Bomb," Ballantine Books, New York, Rev. Ed. 1971.

APPROACH ASSESSMENT

Approach assessment, as well as solution assessment, can occur both before and after we put our carefully chosen solution into effect. Prior to implementation it is a check to see that the best possible effort has been made. After implementation it becomes a detailed follow-up to see if there is anything to be put right or improved. Assessing our overall approach helps us prepare and execute better strategies and solutions the next time around. Some patience is called for here, because insight into our own problem-solving style is not easy to attain. However, with the help of the observations of others, and continuing problem-solving experience, patterns gradually start to emerge. Then we can begin to modify our approach.

THE STRATEGY ELEMENTS

Having split the problem-solving process into these major areas, we can continue a little further with this hierarchic scheme. It can be appreciated that in different problem situations different parts of the problem will require different emphases and effort. These will vary according to the nature of the problem. We cannot apply a blanket approach to all problems. What we need to manage problems success-fully is a building block approach. To introduce some flexibility into the process, we can break the problem-solving divisions down even further. With the building blocks so produced we can quickly make different groupings of problem-solving phases for the different prob-lems we encounter.

In the approach adopted in this book, the problem-solving process is broken down into 38 different "strategy elements." A strategy ele-ment is a small component of problem solving and is composed of groups of questions we might ask at that particular phase of our prob-lem solving efforts.

The strategy element names are listed below. Each strategy ele-ment is described in Chapter 6. The strategy elements with the full listings of questions are contained in Chapter 7.

The use of these strategy elements is shown in the next chapter, where the strategy-building technique will be worked through in detail.

Strategy Element Names:

1. Initial assessment.

2. Set project or solution objectives.

3. Plan organization of operation.

4. Select appropriate techniques.

5. Set up project team.

6. Project into the future.

7. Set standards and success criteria.

8. Question assumptions.

9. Devise appropriate tests.

10. Assess approach so far.

11. Basic fact finding.

12. Available knowledge review.

13. Look at the history of the situation.

14. Determine objectives implicit in the situation.

15. Determine information and decision-making structures.

16. Examine parts and interrelationships.

17. Look at neighboring systems.

18. Assess system needs, resource consumption.

19. Assess demands upon the system.

20. Examine overall structure or system.

21. Fact questioning and assessment.

22. Rearrange to provoke ideas.

23. Take a different approach.

24. Look for similar situations.

25. Juggle, juxtapose, and fantasize.

26. Synthesize.

27. Develop ideas into solutions.

28. Devise information and decision-making routes.

29. Build model of the situation.

30. Initial assessment of solution.

31. Determine implications and ramifications.

32. Attempt improvement.

33. Prepare implementation plans.

34. Project the solution into the future.

35. Assess energy and contribution of the solution.

36. Assess impact and weaknesses of the solution.

37. Check results of the solution.

38. Assess merits and defects of this strategy.

Chapter 3

Building from Basics

From Chapter 2 we know that every problem shares a number of common stages. Yet from our experience we know that every problem presents us with different difficulties. In this chapter we will show how similarities of structure can guide us in producing a problem plan. At the same time we will show how this plan can be adapted to the peculiarities of each problem.

So let us apply the principles outlined so far, and look at a practical example. Since most of us at some point or another become dissatisfied with our life style, or lose our bearings, it might be helpful to look at a strategy for solving the problem of "What shall I do?" With a little ingenuity this strategy could also be applied to corporate objectives. This strategy is laid out in its full form, in the way in which it might be used in a practical situation, in Chapter 5.

In the procedure that follows we first arrange the problem-solving phases to form an outline. Second, we turn this into a skeleton plan, by adapting and labelling those phases and describing them so that they fit our particular situation. Third, we select the strategy elements to add to this skeleton. Fourth, we select specific question groups or questions from the strategy elements. Lastly, we develop and adapt the questions to our situation as required.

THE PROBLEM SOLVING OUTLINE

In the same way that we can home in on a problem's solution, we can home in on the approach to a problem. The key to this is a top-down, or hierarchic, method.

36

In building our approach hierarchically we can start at the top by considering the arrangement of the major problem-solving phases in relation to our particular problem. So first we make a fitting arrangement of the phases of planning, diagnosing, idea generation, solution building, solution assessment, and approach assessment.

As mentioned in Chapter 1, it is a good idea to take a preliminary run through the whole problem-solving sequence to get a firm grasp of the problem. To achieve this the first components of our plan can be: planning, diagnosis, idea generation, solution building, solution assessment. In this way we can make a preliminary exploration of the situation. What we achieve here is both a clearer perception of our real potential and location in the world around us, and a psychological limbering up. In this first stage, however, we would not wish to implement any solutions we may have thought of. Instead we should return to consider further solutions, and only after these had been carefully assessed would we be inclined to undertake any action. To do this we would add on further components: idea generation, solution building, solution assessment. Then, once we have some reasonable solutions, we may try out our solutions in real life and examine

what happened as a result. We represent this process in our plan by including: implement, solution assessment, approach assessment.

Depending on the real life results we may want to re-enter the problem-solving process at some point. If we really do not think we have solved anything, then we would want to start from the very beginning. If we think we are on the right track, but have not been too practical, we may wish to restart at the point of solution building. Or, of course, we may be quite pleased with the results and move on to other challenges. So now we have a vague skeleton which looks like this:

Plan (P)

Diagnose (D)

Idea generation (IG)

Solution building (SB)

Solution assessment (SA)

Idea generation (IG)

Solution building (SB)

Solution assessment (SA)

Implement

Solution assessment (SA

Approach assessment (AA)

A SKELETON PLAN

To turn this outline into a skeleton plan more fitting to our situation we must be a little more specific. As a first step we can label the steps we will be taking, with a very brief title or description. This is the top level of the hierarchical planning procedure. We break the approach down into problem-solving phases which we label and describe specifically. These are later to be broken down into smaller units, as we shall see.

What will we do under "planning" in this "What shall I do?" situation? Here, for once, we do not start straight away with a clearly stated and detailed objective, as this is exactly what we are feeling our way toward, and what will occupy our attention in the diagnosis stage. However, we can have a stateable objective for the project itself. This can be: to derive a clear, satisfactory, fruitful set of objectives for ourselves—or our corporation, business, or other venture—in the context of a rewarding life-style. So, beyond this statement, the planning stage is limited to the construction of the problem-solving approach—which is what we are doing right now.

In the diagnosis stage what will we be doing? To develop a life style we need to locate our potential and reconcile this with our ideal wishes. It is also encouraging and productive for a person to consider, in the initial stages at least, just the good potential. To dwell on our failings at this point is not conducive to imaginative speculation.

So in defining or diagnosing where we are and where we might like to go, the following steps are suggested as the first three in a more specific skeleton. We break the diagnosis stage into three steps since diagnosis is a particularly important phase in this problem situation.

1. **(D)** Find your good points, potential and talents. Look where you have been.

2. **(D)** Consider how these good points could grow.

3. **(D)** Consider where you would like to go ideally.

Having done this gives us some material to think about, and now, having determined and stated as clearly as possible the contents and scope of our problem, we are ready to think up some ideas. We now move into the idea generation phase of our problem solving plan. This can be step 4.

4. **(IG)** Imaginatively reconcile your ideal or desirable objective with your good points.

Step 4 will take a little time, as we ponder our position and then try to get into a relaxed frame of mind to incubate and stimulate ideas.

From here we will want to move on to some means of developing and implementing the ideas from step 4, so we need to take the time to think out and to build well-developed solutions. Step 5 becomes the solution-building phase of the first part of our skeleton.

5. **(SB)** Produce realistic plans.

The next stage is to look at these plans in detail. Are they really any good? Now we are into the solution assessment phase.

6. **(SA)** Assess your plans.

The seventh step is a decision point. Here we decide whether—
even though this is just the first run through our problem—we have
produced a plan which is good enough to be put into effect. If so we
can move onto the later stages of our plan. Otherwise we will carry on
with step 8. So, for a moment, step 7 can be left as:

7. Plans acceptable?

According to our initial skeleton our next move is to generate ideas
and build solutions again. To a large extent the first phases were to
familiarize us with the problem area and get us mentally limbered up.
Now that we have our second wind we can run those first laps again
more spiritedly. So we now try for some better resolution of our

---

SAMPLE PROBLEM PLAN OUTLINE

Formal problem management may seem unnecessarily precise or constraining. Here
are a problem plan for a typical decision and one result of failing to plan.
Problem: Management wants to close down all steel plate stores at all decentralized
factory locations except one. This one is to supply all plate to other factories' field
contract jobs around the country and overseas.

Problem plan outline:
1. **Plan:** Plan coordination of operation with each factory manager, the
   decision-making process for where the surviving plate store is to be, and the
   mechanics of closing down the others.
2. **Define:** State clearly the size and scope of the problem and the ins and outs of
   the decision to close down all the stores.
4. **Idea generation:** Consider possible solutions and select best methods to execute this decision.
5. **Solution building:** Construct detailed plan of action.
6. **Solution assessment:** All managers should examine, review, rework, and
   agree.
7. **Implement.**
8. **Solution assessment:** Review and follow up.

One reason often advanced for not planning carefully is that "Nobody would be so
stupid as to......" However, failure to follow a conscious or formal decision-making
procedure led one company to close down *all* its plate stores when each manager
acted independently and on cost considerations. The cost factor was quickly rein-
troduced as penalty clauses on contract work appeared, when the plate ran out and
stores had to be restocked—too late.

Figure 1

difficulties. Step 8 can be as follows, covering both solution building and idea generation:

8. (**IG,SB**) Attempt to build more rewarding, more fulfilling plans.

The next step can go back to an earlier point, since we now have to assess ideas again as in step 6. So we return to step 6, assess any new plan, then decide its acceptability, as in 7. If acceptable, we move on to step 10 and implement our plan. So the next two steps would look as follows:

9. (**SA**) Assess any new plan. (Return to 6).

10. Implement.

We now have only two steps left in our outline plan, and these both deal with assessing the outcome. The first, step 11, deals with examining the results of the steps we have taken and so is concerned with solution assessment. Here we also reflect upon our whole approach to the problem. The last step, 12, is to decide whether to re-enter the problem-solving process, and, if so, at what point. Thus:

11. (**SA,AA**) Assess the outcome.

12. Next step? (Satisfied? If not, return to 1 or 5).

DEVELOPING THE SKELETON

Now that we have a skeleton plan which follows the principal stages of problem solving and includes a few cycles to maximize our effectiveness, we can start to consider each step in more detail. We have given labels to each step. With these as a guide we can look more closely at what we expect to achieve at each of these points. After this we can continue our hierarchic breakdown of the problem approach by splitting these labelled steps into smaller parts and introducing strategy elements. The principal objective at this stage is to give thought to what is involved in each step and prepare ourselves for selecting suitable strategy elements. The expanded step descriptions should reflect this thinking. With a little thought we might come up with expansions like the following:

1. Think hard to discover your good points. Use some imagination, brainstorm, remember, ask other people. Look at what you have done, what you may have achieved, and what you have enjoyed in the past. Everyone has some strong point. You may surprise yourself.

2. Think how your good points or potential good points might be developed. What could you make them turn into? How could you become better at what you are good at?

3. What would you like to do? What kind of a situation do you wish to work toward? If you don't have any dreams, generate ideas based on your good points and/or any conceivable opportunities. Where do you want to get? How do you want to get there? Develop some ideal objectives.

4. How might you adapt what you would like to do to fit your good points in practice? Can you satisfy the objectives you have in mind in a way which builds upon your strengths? If you do not seem to be able to achieve your dreams, is there something that might substitute? Perhaps you can arrive at some intermediate stage that might help you in a later new attempt at the ideal? Develop some personally realistic objectives.

5. How might you put this into effect? What practical steps might you take to make your objectives attainable? Try to maintain a balance between aiming so high that you will be discouraged by complete failure, or so low that you will not be challenged and your successes seem trivial and unrewarding.

6. How realistic, appropriate, and rewarding are your plans? Here you want to avoid doing things that will fall foul of your weaker points. Now make sure your plans take account of any of your less strong points.

7. If acceptable, go to step 10. Otherwise, if any improvement might be made, carry on with step 8.

8. Now that you have worked your way through your aspirations and difficulties to some kind of plan, sit back and think it over calmly and without pressure. Perhaps daydream a little. Can you now push for something more appealing?

9. Return to step 6 to reassess any new plan.

10. Now start to put your plan into effect. Keep your eye on it. Watch closely to see if things are going according to plan, and be ready to respond to any problems that may turn up. There are always teething troubles to be dealt with, so do not be upset when they appear.

11. Your plans may not have turned out exactly as you had hoped, or the situation may have altered drastically. You may now want to modify your plans, or you may just want to record your experiences for next time. Or you may want to start over.

12. If you want to start all over again, go to step 1. If you want to modify your plans, to go step 5. Otherwise, this is the last point in the process—for now.

Obviously we cannot come up with a skeleton like the above without giving it serious thought and perhaps doing some preliminary investigation or looking at what others have done. So it does need effort. However, unless we take our problem solving seriously and are prepared to pitch in, we will get solutions to our problems which are as wishy-washy as the effort made to solve them.

ADDING IN THE STRATEGY ELEMENTS

In the preceding section we constructed a rough skeleton. This is composed of a generalized problem-solving form which has been adapted to our particular situation. Now we have to think more carefully about the details of our problem and what we will have to do to deal with it. We must consider whether to spend our major efforts in diagnosis, design, or implementation, or whether these all require equal emphasis.

Having done this, we can select some strategy elements and begin to turn them into an action plan. We now begin to concern ourselves a little more with balance, ensuring that in each major step there is some sprinkling of the imaginative to balance the critical, and vice versa.

At the beginning of this chapter—"The problem-solving outline"—we determined the sequence of the problem-solving phases. We can use these phase labels—planning, diagnosing, and so on—as a guide for selecting our strategy elements. In the second part of the book the strategy elements are arranged consecutively in their approximate sequence in the problem-solving process. Each strategy element is labelled with the phase or phases to which it belongs. As there is inevitably some overlap, a separate index is given in Section II of the book of all the elements, under the headings of planning, diagnosing, idea generation, and so on. This can be consulted as we build or add to our skeleton.

Let us now see how we can add strategy elements to the skeleton we have so far.

EXAMPLE OF A FIRST RUN THROUGH A PROBLEM.
How my cartoon strip "Bottom Drawer" *began to take shape.*

---

1. Define problem (use questions from strategy element 1):

1–1. What is the overall problem?
To design a new cartoon strip for an office management magazine to pinpoint various relevant issues in an appealing way.

1–2. Can this be broken into sub-problems?

Devise title

Characters

Theme

Relevance, appeal

2. Generate ideas (use questions from strategy element 23):

2–1. Pursue some initial ideas.

2–1–1. Devise title.

Office Antics

Office Insects

Bureaugnats

Office Overgrowth

Office Undergrowth

Bottom Drawer

2–1–2. Characters.

Animated telephone

Rubber Stamp

Dilly the Dictaphone

Flashy the microfiche

Old Quill the Pen

Elephants

Mice

Birds

Lobsters

Crabs

etc.....

Figure 2

Step 1. (Diagnosis) "Find your good points, potential, talents. See where you have been."

Bearing in mind our expansion of this step, let us look at the diagnosis strategy elements, either by using the index at the beginning of Section II or by going through the strategy element descriptions in Chapter 6. From these we might select element 11, "Basic fact finding," to get us started on digging for our good points. Element 13, "Look at the history of the situation," should let us look into our past. We can attach these strategy element numbers and their titles to our skeleton.

Step 2. (Diagnosis) "How could these good points grow?"

Although we are still looking carefully at ourselves and our potential there is room for a little speculative thought at this point. So we can begin on firm ground by including element 6, "Project into the future," to gain some preliminary projections of where our talents might take us. We may then try to be a little more imaginative about

our future. Element 25, "Juggle, juxtapose, and fantasize," should assist us in breaking out of old ruts in our thinking. Element 24, "Look for similar situations," can be added to provide further expansion of the viewpoints which we might take. Here it can be seen how imaginative elements can be introduced quite early in the process of solving a problem, even before the problem is clearly defined.

Step 3. (Diagnosis)   "Where would you like to go ideally?"

Here we begin to try to give some form to our projected future, however idealistic. Once again element 25 may help us fantasize and juggle possibilities, and element 6 may help extend our thinking in time. But now we also have to formalize this thinking somewhat and come to a clear definition of the problem we are dealing with. Element 2, "Set project or solution objectives," can help us develop our thinking into action goals. Now we should have some idea of the general situation in which we find ourselves.

Step 4. (Idea generation)   "Imaginatively reconcile the ideal or desirable with your good points."

Now we really have to put in some imaginative effort to conceive of how we might attain our ideal goals in the hard and practical everyday world. Here we select from a number of the idea generation strategy elements in hopes of promoting some new and fruitful ideas. We can use parts of elements 22, "Rearrange to provoke ideas," 23, "Take a different approach," 24, "Look for similar situations," and 25, "Jug-

---

SAMPLE ANSWER AT STRATEGY ELEMENT LEVEL.
Adapted from an actual airline systems problem situation.

Strategy Element 2. Set project or solution objectives.

The purpose of this feasibility study is to investigate the activities involved in processing airline tickets, with a view to trying to reduce or not increase staff in ticket handling in the future, and to derive the financial benefits associated with improved timeliness and accuracy in inter-airline billing. Potential savings of unclaimed, earned, inter-airline revenue are in the region of $3½ million. The required benefits are to be achieved without merely shifting the burden to some other department.

Figure 3

gle, juxtapose, and fantasize." Then, with the idea pot nicely bubbling, we can begin to coax out some original syntheses. To do this we can make use of element 26, "Synthesize." Then we have to revert to a more practical level by developing or modifying some coherent objectives using element 2 again, "Set project or solution objectives."

Step 5. (Solution building)   "Produce realistic plans."

Now that we have what we think are fairly realistic goals for our lives, how are we going to achieve them? We need an action plan. We must translate our intentions into observable real world activity. What is the shape of this activity to be? In this step we must select, not too heavily, from quite a large number of strategy elements. This section is one of those mini-problem-solving cycles which we mentioned earlier.

One of the first things we must do is to convert our goals into some observable success criteria. We need some pre-arranged indicators to tell us when we have arrived. Strategy element 7 will be a first selection, "Set standards and success criteria."

Next we should take a slightly closer look at some of the implications and ramifications of our proposed goals. Once again we can use element 11, "Basic fact finding," to hunt for more detail where this can be seen to be needed. Element 12, "Available knowledge re-

---

SAMPLE DELIBERATIONS AT STRATEGY ELEMENT LEVEL.
Adapted from a heavy electrical engineering contractor's problem situation

---

Element 31. Consider implications and ramifications.

In considering a new Stores Control and Records system, one of the factors to be considered in designing the system was one most people had forgotten:

What will be the effect of future metrification plans?

Will we have to keep stocks of both metric and standard plate and pipe sizes for different contracts?

What will this do to stores costs in terms of space, handling, record maintenance, stock on hand, etc.?

How will we make the transition?

How long will it take?

Figure 4

view," can help by getting us to look at the experiences of others who have followed our road, or similar pathways. Element 16, "Examine parts and interrelationships," can assist our attempts to ferret out intricacies and inconsistencies. Element 20, "Examine overall structure or system," will aid us in looking at the total picture as well as the pieces.

Having done this, we need to take thought and introduce a critical attitude for a time. Begin with selections from element 21, "Fact questioning and assessment." Then probe a little more deeply with element 8, "Question assumptions." Next, look for hidden motivations more carefully, using element 14, "Determine objectives implicit in the situation." Here a fine balance of assessment and imagination is called for to check out exactly what would be the most appropriate for us.

We should now have a clearer picture of our requirements, and can once again slip back into an imaginative frame of mind as we ponder plans. Once more we can select from 22, 23, 24, 25, and 26 to assist the quest for appealing and practical routes to our goals.

Now comes a more serious and practical effort to pull all the pieces together into a plan that will survive in real life. To organize the events and actions required we use element 3, "Plan organization of the operation." If we combine this with element 27, "Develop ideas into solutions," we will help pin down any fuzzy areas and lay out the skeleton of an action plan. Then we follow this with element 33, "Prepare implementation plans," to work out the exact details of what we will do.

Step 6. (Solution assessment)   "Assess your plans."

If *at all* possible, we must let our ideas sit for a period. We should try to arrange things so that we can get on with some other activity for awhile. One way of gaining perspective is to allow time to pass. This is important. Even if it is just overnight we ought to try to let some interval elapse before we resume work. There are any number of occasions where this may not be possible, although a little ingenuity can occasionally gain us some time. In this instance, we are dealing with a fairly long-term project and so the problem-solving activity can be comparatively leisurely.

Having left the project alone briefly, let us now look at appropriate elements for assessment. A good starting point would be element 30, "Initial assessment of solution." This can be followed with a closer look by using 31, "Determine implications and ramifications," and 16, "Examine parts and interrelationships." Element 34, "Project solution into the future," can give us a longer-term view of affairs. To examine the situation from a slightly different angle, we might select element 10, "Assess approach so far." The use of element 34 brings a little imagination to temper the otherwise severely analytic slant of this step.

Step 7. (Decision point/assessment)   "Plans acceptable?"

If the plans appear flawless and not capable of improvement, we can go to step 10 and implement them. Otherwise we continue with step 8 to improve good plans or straighten out wrinkles in less good plans. Of course, if the plans have turned out to be hopeless, we may want to return to step 5 and produce a new set.

Step 8. (Idea generation and solution building)   "Improve plans."

Here the emphasis is on improvement, so a liberal addition of imagination is called for, though with a practical bias. A useful element here would be 32. "Attempt improvement." To support this element we need to look for some new perspectives, so it might help to add element 23, "Take a different approach." Element 26, "Synthesize," can be used to tie together any new conceptions we may think of. To rebuild the solution and prepare for action we can use element 27, "Develop ideas into solutions."

Step 9. (Decision point/assessment)   "Assess any new plan."

If we produced something different in step 8, however small that difference, we must reassess the plans. Often a tiny, apparently insignificant change can cause disaster. So let's avoid that possibility and return to step 6. Otherwise we can pass on to step 10.

Step 10. (Action)   "Implement."

As we set our plans in motion we need to keep an eye on them. Selections from two elements will help here. Element 10, "Assess approach so far," and element 3, "Plan organization of the operation," contain some question groups appropriate to this stage of the operation.

Step 11. (**Solution assessment/approach assessment**) "Assess Outcome."

In looking back on our efforts two elements can help us judge both the solution's outcome and our competence in putting it all together. These are 37, "Check results of Soluttion," and 38, "Assess merits and defects of this strategy." Here we see if we still have further work to do.

Step 12. (**Decision point/assessment**) "Next step?"

If we have been successful, this is the end of the strategy. If not, we will return to step 1, or step 5, whichever is appropriate or possible.

Now let us summarize the skeleton we have built. After this we will look at a way of building a strategy where we are not sufficiently sure of ourselves to think out the kind of outline developed above. Then we will return to developing the "What shall I do?" strategy in detail.

SUMMARY SO FAR

Step Number and Title	Strategy Elements Drawn Upon
1. Find your good points. potential, talents. Look where you have been.	11,13
2. How could these good points grow?	6,25,24
3. Where would you like to go, ideally?	6,25,2
4. Imaginatively reconcile the ideal or desirable with your good points.	22,23,24,25,26
5. Produce realistic plans.	7,11,12,16,20
	21,8,14
	22,23,24,25,26
	3,27,33
6. Assess your plans.	30,31,16,34,10

7. Are your plans acceptable?	Yes: go to step 10.
	No: go to step 8.
8. Attempt to build more rewarding, more fulfilling plans.	32,23,26,27.
9. Assess any new plans.	If new plan, go to step 6.
10. Implement.	10,3.
11. Assess the outcome.	37,38.
12. Next step?	Finish: end.
	Modify: go to step 5.
	Start again: go to step 1.

INTERLUDE—A STARTING PLACE FOR WHEN WE DO NOT KNOW HOW TO START

Developing a skeleton outline in the way demonstrated above may not always come easily. If we cannot operate at that level for some reason, we can start from a basic generalized skeleton and a consid-

eration of the strategy elements themselves. In Chapter 4 we will be looking in detail .at some larger, prestructured skeletons which also obviate the need to build from scratch for certain problem types.

Let us now look at a simple, basic skeleton which can be a starting point for any problem. This skeleton covers each of the problem-solving phases and contains organizational, imaginative, and critical elements.

Stage and Title	Strategy Element Number and Name
Get started. (Plan)	1. Initial assessment. (25. Juggle, juxtapose, fantasize. [optional]). 2. Set project or solution objectives.
2. Clearly define the problem. (Diagnosis)	11. Basic fact finding. 13. Look at the history of the situation. 21. Fact questioning and assessment.
3. Seek imaginative ideas. (Idea generation)	23. Take a different approach. 25. Juggle, juxtapose, and fantasize. 26. Synthesize.
4. Construct solutions out of these. (Solution building)	27. Develop ideas into solutions. 29. Build model of the situation
5. Make implementation plans. (Solution building)	33. Prepare implementation plans.
6. Assess and improve solution. (Solution assessment)	30. Initial assessment of solution. 31. Determine implications and ramifications. 32. Attempt improvement.

7. *Follow-up and approach assess-*   37. Check results of solution.
ment. (Solution assessment and ap-
proach assessment)   38. Assess merits and defects of this
                     approach.

This strategy skeleton is expanded into a usable mini-strategy below.

With this as a starting point we could begin work on an initial assessment to give us a better feeling for the situation, or we could think about the situation and add a few more strategy elements after perusing the strategy element descriptions in Chapter 6. These selections could be made as above.

BREAKING DOWN STRATEGY ELEMENTS INTO QUESTION GROUPS AND QUESTIONS

To return to our sample strategy, we may wish to start work on our problem at this stage, especially if we feel we cannot go any further in detail without some actual exploration. If so, we would follow our outline plan, making use of such guidance as is contained in its form, and in the strategy element descriptions which we have attached to our plan.

Starting work at this point would also be appropriate if the problem to be solved, or the decision to be made, did not warrant spending too much time on it. It may also be appropriate as a first run-through, before building the full strategy with a better feeling for the situation. In this way we will be able to obtain a good enough grasp of the situation to produce a relevant detailed strategy later on, prior to a full scale attack on the problem.

If none of the above reasons apply and we wish to continue more detailed strategy building, we can look more closely at the strategy elements themselves. We can begin to select groups of questions which seem appropriate, and then the specific questions themselves. We may also delay selection of specific questions until we start work on the problem, at that time using whatever questions seem suitable.

We should guard against the impression that the skeleton is fixed, or that particular questions or question groups *must* be used. The skeleton is to give direction; that is all. We must be able to handle this process with a light touch, and not get immersed in so much detail that any incentive to solve the problem evaporates. We must take care to balance the need for speed against being too hasty, and the need for thoroughness against being too ponderous.

So first we pick the question groups which seem suitable. Having decided upon likely-looking question groups, we can then select from these to provide the questions we want for our problem-solving effort. Here we should exercise some care. This is necessary because some of the seemingly less appropriate questions can be the ones which trigger off new insights. Sometimes it pays to think hard about such questions. They may reveal something we failed to connect to our situation. Occasionally we may have to take an entirely different view of our situation just to be able to ask the question. Taking the time to do this could provide new insights.

Sometimes it is hard to resist selecting almost every question—just in case. Unfortunately, when trying to answer these later, enthusiasm can become blunted by the massive effort involved. This is especially so because, if the questions are to be used to advantage, considerable thought must be given to each one. It is suggested that on average no more than two questions from each question group be selected, picking those which seem most stimulating and most likely to get to the heart of the matter. If this does not seem sufficient when we have reached the end of question selection, we can run through again and add as few questions as we can, consonant with thoroughness.

It is better to err on the small side. A paucity of questions will quickly make itself plain as we come to grips with a problem. Then, when we quickly skim our strategy elements for a few extra questions, we will have a better idea of what to look for. If, however, we overload ourselves with questions to start with, motivation will rapidly be lost as we are held back from attacking the problem by a bureaucratic nightmare of turgid questions.

When selecting from the creativity strategy elements such as 22–25, it is also a good idea to take just one or two of the questions or instructions and concentrate on thinking up ideas about them. This can get ideas flowing better than skimming lightly over a number of questions. An optimum number for idea-producing checklists has been found to be seven, but we must do whatever produces the best results for ourselves in terms of the number of ideas generated, and the ease of flow of these ideas.

In using creativity questions we should remember that we do not

---

SAMPLE ANSWER TO STRATEGY QUESTION
Adapted from the airline systems problem situation mentioned in Figure 3.

Strategy Question 11–1–1. What is the overall situation?

An airline ticket can contain many sections relating to different legs of a flight, covering a considerable period of time. When a ticket is produced, an audit slip is detached. This slip contains all flight data but it is not stored at this point for further processing. The information is collected when the individual flight leg slips are returned. As other carriers are often involved, it is necessary to have these slips in order to bill accurately for the flight section covered. These slips often go astray and the carbons themselves are hard to read accurately. The problems resulting here involve refunds, exchanges, medical/legal problems, and a loss of revenue through failing to bill other carriers whose passengers have travelled on this airline's aircraft at some point in their journey.

Figure 5

resist crazy ideas. We set our minds loose; we let the ideas flow. Crazy, wild, silly, or embarrassing ideas can lead to really sensible ideas in some quite roundabout ways. They can spark off useful ideas by drawing attention to a fresh aspect, or by sounding like another word, or by in some other way resembling or triggering something in another area. So we do not stop them. They really can provide short cuts, not always, but often enough to make it all worthwhile. Also, if we are embarrassed by some of the silly things we think of, who but ourselves is to know where the resulting bright ideas came from?

When we select our question groups and questions we need only note their numbers beside their respective strategy elements on our plan. When we have our plan ready for use, we may wish to note down the strategy element descriptions to remind us of the general shape of our strategy. However, the questions themselves can quickly be picked out of the latter half of the book using their identifying numbers. The construction of strategies does not have to become a masssive clerical task.

Let us now look at some strategy question expansions for the example we hve been using in this chapter.

The first strategy element we chose in step 1 of our skeleton was element 11. Suppose we decide that, for a project the size of the one we are working on, question groups 11−1, 11−4, 11−5 and 11−6 are the only really appropriate sets. If we use these question groups we should be able to generate some useful information in relation to our good points—our charge under step 1 of our skeleton.

Which questions might we select from these groups? This will vary with individual cases, but the following might be a typical choice:

From 11—1:

11−1−1. What is the overall situation?

11−1−2. What are the major trends, what are some of the minor trends, what forecasts have been made?

11−1−3. What are the components of this problem? How many are there?

11−1−4. What are the attributes or characteristics of these components?

11−1−5. What are the most significant, important, or urgent aspects of this problem? Why?

From 11—4:

11−4. What is being done?

11−4−1. Why is it being done?

11−4−2. How is it being done?

From 11—5:

11−5. What is happening? What difficulties are there, and what opportunities?

11−5−1. Why is it all happening?

11−5−2. Where is it happening?

11−5−3. When is it happening?

From 11—6:

11−6. What are the major variables and decision sequences?

11−6−2. What attitudes are involved?

11−6−4. What values are involved?

11−6−6. Is there anything, any relationship, value, structural framework, process, or pattern which remains the same over any significant period of time?

11−6−7. What elements or aspects are involved in any pattern you see?

11−6−10. What and where are the strong points?

11−6−11. What have you missed?

We then continue this selection process with the other strategy elements involved in our plan.

ADAPTING QUESTIONS TO SPECIFIC SITUATIONS

Our selected questions can often be put to work without further ado. Sometimes their generalized form might need a little interpretation or reflection before the right questions can be asked.

As an example, let us look at the first question group selected above. We can convert the general questions into the actual questions to which these may conceivably lead when we investigate our good points. In what follows the original questions are given in bold face letters, with the derived questions following in regular type. Needless to say these are not the only interpretations which might be made.

SAMPLE ANSWER TO STRATEGY ELEMENT QUESTION
Adapted from an actual personnel problem situation.

Strategy Element 8. Question assumptions.

Problem: Productivity and morale of the data processing department's keypunchers is low.

Suggested answer: The new line of keypunch machines, which make error correction easier and throughput faster and less tiring, will boost productivity and morale.

8–3–2. Is there a way of leaving the facts the same but seeing them differently?

Perhaps the source of the problem is not morale or productivity, but the role the keypunchers see themselves as playing. Pursuing this line of thought, it was found that the keypunchers had no clear idea of why they were doing their work, nor where they fitted in the organization's work flow, nor what the value of their contribution was. When their role and contribution were made clear to them, their morale and productivity went up.

Figure 6

AN INITIAL ASSESSMENT OF A SITUATION
Adapted from an actual Library information systems problem.

---

1. Initial assessment:

    1–1. What are you trying to do?

        Provide fast, cheap access to public catalogue information on five floors of a building, without the enormous expense of duplicating and maintaining physical card catalogues.

    1–6. How many different kinds of solution to this problem might there be (note that these are *ideas* for solutions, not genuine solutions)?
        1—Massive physical duplication of card catalogue on all floors (rejected).
        2—Conversion of catalogue information to computer records and a computer-produced book catalogue.
        3—Microfilm the catalogue and distribute microfilm copies to each floor.
        4—Hybrid computer/microfilm system using computer-read microfilm as input and computer-produced microfilm as output.

    1–5–5. Can this problem be broken down into smaller parts which can fairly safely be dealt with separately?

The above three projected solutions can be thoroughly investigated and costed out.

    1–7. What is to be done to tackle this problem?

Set up a project group of systems people and librarians to investigate the three alternative possibilities, look for other possibilities, and produce a report recommending a solution and the means of implementing it.

Figure 7

11–1–1. What is the overall situation? What do you consider to be some of the more important things in life? What do you get the most enjoyment out of doing, feeling, or responding to? What do you find rewarding, uplifting, worthwhile?

11–1–2. What are the major trends. What are some of the minor trends? What forecasts have been made? Where do you seem to function well? Where do you seem to function less well? What directions do these qualities seem to be taking? What do other people think you could do well?

11–1–3. What are the components of this problem? How many are there? In how many areas do you function well? What skills, what attitudes, what personal qualities do you do well with? What talents and what potential do you think you have?

11−1−4. **What are the attributes or characteristics of these components?** Go into some detail looking at these good points. How are they good? Why are they good?

11−1−5. **What are the most significant, important or urgent aspects of this problem? Why?** What seem to be your most significant good points? Which are the most valuable to you yourself, to your friends, to the world around you?

The above process of specification can take place as the problem is being worked upon.

Here another characteristic of the generalized strategy questions begins to show itself. The strategy questions act as "seed" questions. In addition to their value as questions in their own right, they may lead us to other significant questions of our own making. Or they may lead us to explore directions we might never otherwise have thought of.

In the above eight sections it can be seen how it is possible to break down a problem from a vague outline to a specific step-by-step plan of action.

All these questions then become tasks to be carried out. In larger projects the various stages in the strategy can be given expected

---

SAMPLE OF DERIVED QUESTIONS
Here 1–1–8 turned out to be quite a fruitful seed question.

Adapted from an actual problem encountered by a systems group at a university installing a computer data base management system.

1–1–8. What issues are you trying to resolve?
This can be answered at various levels from: "Trying to make the best possible use of expensive software," through, "Discovering what the communications problems of promoting DBMS are," to, "Taking the first steps in building a supportive, integrated information and organization tool." This might become a sub-problem: Who thinks what? Whose objectives? Who should have a say in formulating these objectives? Do the people apparently involved share the same picture of the objectives? How do you know? Have you ever really discussed among yourselves the exact nature of your goals, aspirations, objectives, directions? To what extent do these objectives overlap goals in contiguous and in different areas? Can you present a united front? Are any of your objectives in any way inconsistent?

Figure 8

completion dates, staffing requirements, reports to be written, costs and cost estimates to be made, or any other applicable considerations. At this point the use of more formal project management techniques can be made—a step we would presumably have considered if we had incorporated element 4: "Select appropriate techniques."

We should now have something we can use. The complete strategy for our sample problem of this chapter is laid out fully in Chapter 5. At the end of the present chapter there is a list of reminders to help us in our strategy building.

A GENERAL MINI-STRATEGY FOR A FIRST LOOK AT ANY PROBLEM

This is the expanded version of the skeleton introduced above. The numbers in the text are the numbers of the strategy element questions in Chapter 7.

This mini-strategy includes, very close to the start, a set of crazy questions (25−3−9, 25−3−8, 25−1−9) designed to jolt us into a more free-ranging approach to the problem. If these questions are taken seriously and some effort is made to deal with them, this excursion into near-nonsense can have the double benefit of relieving tension or over-motivation, and presenting insights that would otherwise never have surfaced. The hard work of problem solving can then resume with a mind prepared for new and different twists, and a more open approach to defining and resolving the problem.

1.   Get started

Get the feel of the situation. Figure out what you are going to have to do to tackle the problem. If you like, limber up by speculating on some wild solutions.

1−2. What kind of problem is this? For example, is it emotional, political, organizational, theoretical, technical, financial, psychological, medical, or other; or what blend of various factors?

1−2−2. How complex does this problem seem to be? How many parts and levels does it seem to have?

1−3. What seems to be happening? What difficulties are there and what opportunities?

1−3−7. Which seem to be the critical areas?

1−7. What is to be done to tackle this problem? (Here you may wish to use 25−3−9, 25−3−8, and 25−1−9, which also appear below in step 3).

2−1−2. What are your short-term aims?

2−1−3. What are your long-term aims?

2−2−1. What are the specific characteristics of the situation you wish to bring about?

2. Clearly define the problem

Get the real issues straight here. Don't set off with only a vague and hasty perception of the problem.

11−6. What are the major variables and decision sequences?

11−1−8. Does this involve any deeper issues?

13−1−1. How were the present relationships or arrangements of events brought about? How did things get to be this way?

13−2−1. What growth, change, decay, or evolutionary patterns are evident?

13−2−4. Is this situation enmeshed in difficulties of a different kind?

21−1. Why do you perceive this to be a problem? What objectives are being frustrated?

21−1−7. Can you be certain that the problem is what it seems to be?

21−2. Are you sure you have all the information you need?

21−4−1. What is connected to what? Can you draw a map or picture of the pieces? How is each one connected, or how could or should it be, to the others? Are there any missing connections?

21−4−6. Where is all the pressure coming from and why?

21−6−4. Which areas need the most effort, the most time, the most watching, the most thought?

3. Seek imaginative ideas

Try to get your mind moving in new channels. Break out of the immediate confines of the problem and look for new ways of seeing all this.

23−1−1. Is there a different way of describing your objectives? Perhaps a different statement, a different angle, or viewpoint, will lead to different ideas for solutions?

23−2−10. Can you focus on a weakness in your situation and turn it into an unexpected bonus?

23−3−9. What does it look like backwards? Can you turn the situation upside down?

25−3−9. What is the most ridiculous solution you can think of? If you were put in charge of making this solution work sensibly how would you do it? What is the craziest thing you could do or which could happen?

25−3−8. Can you see the humorous side of this? How could you make a joke using parts of this problem? How could you use that?

25−1−9. Can you think of any way at all (think really hard) in which ideas for this situation could be sparked off by thinking about: a button? a candle? a gate? a hinge? a wheel? a can? a bush? meteor? a caterpillar? the sun? an explosion? a river? Select one or two.

26−1−4. What seem to be the key characteristics of this situation? What is the crux of the matter?

26−1−5. What seems to be the most fruitful or rewarding direction to follow? In what areas are ideas or explanations for this likely to be found?

26−1−6. How do you think these things might fit together? Have you a provisional, preliminary feeling for how this goes together?

26−3−5. Is some kind of intermediate stage or idea feasible or advisable?

4. Construct solutions out of these

Take any potentially fruitful ideas, and work them into properly structured solutions. Explore the ins and outs.

27−3−1. What will be the component parts of your new situation? Have you specified these?

27−3−2. What are your targets, what time is required, what are your deadlines and priorities?

27−3−3. What are your alternate plans and priorities, what are your emergency plans?

27−4−3. Do any other things need to happen to make your solution possible? If so how are you going to ensure that they do?

29−1−2. Can you lay out a hierarchical structure or breakdown of possible choices and outcomes?

29−1−3. Can you list the decisions to be made in various circumstances?

29−1−4. Can you assign a degree of risk or uncertainty to the choice points?

5. Make implementation plans

Detail how you plan to actually do something with this solution. How will you put it into effect and keep it that way?

33-1. How do you plan to transfer your solution from your head, or from paper, to real life?

33-1-6. How are future developments likely to affect this system?

33-2-1. What areas are there?

33-2-5. What activities have important sequencing or timing constraints? What is the best sequencing and timing of these?

33-3-1. What steps and stages are required? What will you do if these get out of joint?

33-4. What progress checkpoints will there be?

33-4-9. Imagine a disaster for your solution. How would you avoid it?

6. Assess and improve your solution

Now pick holes in it and try to make it all into a superior solution.

30-1-1. Are you sure this is what you really want or what is really needed?

30-1-5. Has this been thoroughly thought through?

30-1-4. Where are the greatest risks? Where are the greatest challenges? Can these be handled?

30-3-2. Are you looking at more than one solution seriously—or have you rushed for the one which seems to solve the most immediate aspects of the problem.?

30-2-4. Is any part of the situation or solution in conflict with, or likely to be in conflict with, any other part?

31-3-1. To what degree is this linked to, approaching, or on a collision-course with anything else?

31-4. Have you analyzed the various solutions proposed in respect of any trade-offs which may have to be made?

32-1. How can this be made more effective? More powerful? More significant?

32-1-6. How can this be made by more stimulating? How can this be made more motivating?

32-3-1. Now that you have found the obvious solution, can you find one which is less obvious?

7. Follow-up and approach assessment

What do you think of your solution and of your performance? What have you learned? Did it work as you thought?

37–1–1. If the solution failed, can it be patched up until a new one is ready?

37–1–3. If the solution failed, was it completely inadequate and out of touch with the reality of the situation?

37–1–4. If the solution failed, has it upset anything else and, if so, what will you do about it?

37–2–1. Has the solution or its effects presented any new opportunities? If so, what can be done to exploit these?

37–2–4. Was the solution worth the effort? Was the effort disproportionate to the value of the solution?

37–3–8. Is the solution going to continue working like this, or is something going to go wrong sooner or later?

38–1–1. What and where are the strong points? What do you think the good points about your approach have been? Efficiency? Speed? Interest? Enjoyment?

38–1–2. What and where are the weak points? What do you think the bad points about your approach have been? Wrong direction? Too cumbersome? Disorganized? Uninspired?

38–2–7. Did you minimize the activities which did not contribute directly to overall objectives? Did you maximize those which did?

38–3. Was this the most effective way to do this? Was this the best action you could have taken?

38–4. How can you benefit from this situation for similar situations in the future?

KEEPING STRATEGY BUILDING IN PERSPECTIVE

Part of the skill involved in building a strategy is to ensure that our approach is appropriate to the situation with which we are dealing. Let us look at this a little more closely.

In some particularly fast-moving, changeable, turbulent, or unformed situation our strategy may need to change as fast as we make it. In these kinds of situations it may sometimes be better to pick out strategy elements whenever they seem to be applicable, and use them as checklists. In a difficult situation we may not have time to figure out a full-blown approach, but we may appreciate a list of questions that we can work through to assist our assessment of the situation, for example, and to prevent our forgetting an obvious question which we would have thought of had things not been so hectic, stressful, or just too fast-moving. When our minds are spinning, the strategy questions can give us useful back-up. But whatever the situation, some guiding values or objectives are needed to provide coherence.

As we manage to pin the situation down and begin to get a better grasp of it, we may set up a skeleton strategy, perhaps just working on the strategy element descriptions. Then as we finally get time to deal with the situation more forcefully, we can prepare a full-size strategy. However, if the situation is not completely out of our grasp, and if we have at least 24 hours or so in which to solve our problem, then it would be beneficial to spend an hour producing a strategy and starting to pull the situation—or at least what we perceive to be the next phase of the situation—together in a fairly methodical and reasonably controlled manner.

The more slow-moving the situation, the more time we will have to plan the whole project in advance. However, since the problem continues while we work on our strategy, this does not provide us with an excuse to spend all our time planning and no time in doing. The strategy-building process permits us to put together effective strategies more quickly and to come to grips with the complexities of the situation sooner.

Modifying the Approach

As work on the problem proceeds, it may be necessary to alter the kind of strategy used, if the situation is perceived to change. The important thing is not to use an approach suitable for one type of situation when we are dealing with another. If we use a highly structured strategy in a fast-moving and risky situation we will soon find ourselves overwhelmed by unpredicted changes. If we use a pure checklisting approach in more slow-moving conditions we will waste a great deal of time, probably lose control of the situation, and miss the opportunity to produce coherent, suitably structured, and precise solutions.

The strategies are not meant to constrain but to guide. If in the process of using a strategy, there appears a better route or a sudden new perception, steps in the strategy can be omitted, or the strategy can be redesigned or abandoned. The strategies are tools to help explore, discover, and provide speedy guides to support this activity on a larger scale, or in more complex situations than would otherwise be feasible.

With the aid of the strategy-building process we should be able to tackle bigger problems, and to do it with more confidence and more success.

The discipline of working through a problem situation point by point soon reveals any fuzziness in our conception of what we are doing, any vagueness in why we are doing it, or what it is all about. This may reveal unwarranted assumptions. As we are forced by answering the questions to clarify and question, we soon form a clearer, deeper picture of the situation and some of the obstacles, and possible courses of action are uncovered.

One thing which soon becomes apparent when using the strategy-generating technique is that our minds keep thinking of answers or difficulties in stages of the problem which we are not currently working on. These questions should not be disciplined into place. Rather they should be quickly noted at their appropriate places in the skeleton, and either explored or left before we return to our place in the procedure.

How Big Is a Strategy?

In building our first strategies it is probably a good idea to start small. Look at the mini-strategies in Chapter 4, for example. These permit us to tackle quickly parts of projects of fairly small size. They contain only 50 or 60 questions. When we start putting strategies together, it is tempting to include more elements and questions than we really need. As a result of the secure feeling of having covered all angles to a problem, we are then faced with the heroic task of answering all the questions. So it is a good exercise to attempt to produce a thorough problem-solving plan with a minimum of questions. Fit the number of the questions to the size or importance of the problem and the time available.

Obviously a large, complex, long-drawn-out project would benefit from a larger set of questions, but speed and flexibility should always be a goal. The 50- or 60-question strategy should suffice for the mini-project. Perhaps 150 to 200 for a medium-sized project, and a target size of 350 for larger projects might be advisable.

Later, when our strategies begin to be made up very quickly using a series of our favorite mini-strategies instead of the basic strategy elements, we quickly run into size problems. We may have to do some cautious paring down of these high-level strategy elements. If this seems counter-productive, we will have to develop the skill of speedily skimming for significant questions.

We should not forget that the strategy questions act as "seed" questions, and further questions will spring to mind as we employ our strategies. Too many of the "seed" questions will rapidly cause mental indigestion, or alternatively dull the very thinking processes that the strategy-building process is supposed to free us to exercise. Also the strategy element descriptions alone often contain their own seed questions, and may provide enough detail for certain projects.

Remaining Flexible

The strategy-generation process emphasizes careful analysis of objectives and painstakingly working through a carefully constructed program. This may seem to conflict with the meanings of "flexibility" and "innovation," and with the frequent need in real life for approximation, adaptation, best-guessing, and see-what-happens attitudes. However, it must be appreciated that: first, the clear analysis and understanding of overall objectives make possible quick accommodation when lesser objectives are thwarted; second, "Assessment of approach so far" is a very important feedback element, the use of which can drastically reorient projects. Since it refers back to basic objectives, this will not produce arbitrary or seat-of-the-pants firefighting; third, the very purpose of the check-listing style is to allow more precise and painstaking work to be accomplished in less time, and thus permit more flexible, adaptive, and exploratory behavior overall; fourth, there is no reason why this whole procedure should be employed unimaginatively.

As with all tools that provide structure, the building of strategies must be handled lightly, lest it enmesh us in bureaucratic rigidity.

The trouble with developing a productive problem-solving style, or of developing a successful approach to a particular range of problems, is that the very success of the method may upset the novelty/ routine balance. On the one hand, we need to strive to raise skills from the level of struggling to the level of competence so that we can build on them and develop further. On the other hand, we must guard against letting our overall style coagulate and produce a rigid, unquestioning mental bureaucracy. Once a problem area has been mastered and controlled, a great deal of the innovative, exploratory dynamism, as well as the risk-taking, conflict and stress, is missing from our next approach to it. As a result, we may have a side-effect of reduced awareness, reduced sensitivity to anomalies in situations, and reduced ability to pick up on inconsistencies or to extend our thinking into new areas.

To assist in striking a balance between starting afresh every day and dropping into a deadly routine, the "Assess approach" phase should be tagged onto each problem-solving effort. Then we might pay more attention to the balance involved and be less likely to have our thinking become routine.

Skipping Around Levels

In adapting a skeleton to a particular situation, we may find ourselves using the strategy at a number of different levels. Some of the time we may be thinking about the problem only at the level of the title of the section—that is, taking a very broad and cursory view. At other parts of the process we may be working question by question through a strategy element group. In some parts we may never even get beyond the broadest consideration of that section of the problem, simply because it is not necessary or appropriate to do so. At other times we may be plodding along at a very detailed level indeed.

If we have constructed a strategy which we subsequently find to be either too detailed or not detailed enough, the hierarchic structuring will help. If it is too detailed, we can leave out the most detailed levels. If it is not detailed enough, we can add an extra level of questions as we work through each section. In both cases we take our cues from the actual problem as we get the feel of it. However, we must be careful not to panic and pull our strategy to pieces.

Simplifying is really important in strategy building. We must avoid clumsy, over-elaborate structures. The reason for having labels for our steps in the strategy is to facilitate the hierarchical grouping and breaking down of a strategy into stages more easily remembered than strings of strategy elements. As we build more involved strategies, we must make sure that we keep grouping areas under meaningful labels and then grouping groups, and so on, so that the strategy still breaks down into pieces we can handle. Even a complex structure can be simplified by a hierarchical arrangement or by the combination of an iterative process with a hierarchical structure of levels.

We should not lose the driving power, the excitement of the new idea, or the advantages of striking fast and first. But we must not rush off with an idea, with lots of loose ends dangling, which could be made much better—just for the sake of a small victory now—and sacrifice a larger victory later.

STRATEGY BUILDER'S CHECKLIST

This provides some pointers to bear in mind while building our strategy. We could, if we wished, expand upon this by drawing upon some of the questions under strategy element 10, "Assess approach so far," or strategy element 38, "Assess merits and defects of this strategy."

While building our strategy—

1. Can I go any further with this strategy at this point?

2. Should I wait until I find out more about this situation?

3. Have I planned as far as it is possible to plan?

4. If my strategy is incomplete, do I have a reserve plan to fall back on in case of emergency?

5. Do circumstances dictate that I quickly put a provisional solution into effect until a rigorous analysis and thorough problem-solving effort can take place?

6. Is this both imaginative and practical?

7. Is this both well organized and adaptable?

8. Can this be easily broken down into stages or sections?

9. Does this reflect all the stages of the problem-solving process?

10. Is there an overall balance of all the parts of this strategy?

Before we use our strategy—

1. Is this the most effective way to do this?

2. Is there any point at which it could be improved? Be made more imaginative? Quicker? More flexible? More appealing?

3. Can I eliminate the weaknesses?

4. Can I improve its strengths?

5. Do I have a clear enough grasp of what I am trying to do that I can remain in control of the situation when things become complicated or confusing?

6. Is this the same tired old approach?

7. Is it too complicated?

8. Is this attempting too much; procrastinating; avoiding difficulties; unethical?

9. Is this unrealistic, impractical; overcomplicated; simplistic; unfruitful?

10. Is this uncontrollable; facing overwhelming opposition; inappropriate; badly timed?

SUMMARY OF THE STRATEGY BUILDING PROCESS–BUILDING FROM SCRATCH

1. Think about your problem. Mull it over; get into the frame of mind for tackling it.

2. Bearing in mind the problem management principles (Chapter 1), the basic problem solving stages (Chapter 2), and some of the different styles of approach (Chapter 3), chop your problem up into some convenient-sized pieces. You may wish to use headings like: "Get straight what is going on," "Clarify issues involved," "Produce imaginative alternatives," "Develop tentative solutions," and so on.

3. Go through the list of strategy element descriptions (Chapter 6) and pick out those which you think can be used in your basic framework.

4. Attach the numbers of the strategy elements you choose to your headings, in the sequence in which you think they will fit best. Some elements may appear in several places. Samples of skeletons can be seen in Chapter 4.

5. When you have formed a skeleton plan, use the strategy element numbers or titles to select some strategy element questions. These are to be found in Chapter 7, a set of pages for each strategy element.

6. Pick the groups of questions which you want and add their numbers to your skeleton plan. You may not wish to use all the groups of a particular strategy element. Select those that seem fitting.

7. Run through the strategy as it appears in its full form. Think about it. You may wish at this point to use strategy element 10 or 38 to assist you, or to be guided by the strategy builder's checklist in the previous section, above. You may next wish to regroup, add, subtract, rearrange, or in some other way modify your strategy.

8. When you have your strategy finalized, modify your skeleton accordingly and make sure you have noted down element group or page numbers.

9. Now you are ready to go.

Chapter 4

Expandable Models

To some extent, stating overall principles or a general pattern of productive thinking, though important, falls short of giving real assistance to the problem solver who faces a practical difficulty. In real life, problem solving takes many twists and turns. The path to a solution in one instance may only bear a faint resemblance to that taken in a different instance. Despite overall similarities in psychological structure or theoretical form, the artist and the businessman in practice do different things when they solve problems. If we are not to start from bare basics with each and every problem—which could be a time-consuming prospect—something a little closer to an employable plan would be an advantage.

FLEXIBLE MODELS

The strategy-building technique presented in this book provides elements which can be built into any kind of a plan. If we do not want to start from basics each time using a great many pieces, we can instead select a halfway point. We can make use of a skeleton which is fairly clearly directed to a particular type of problem, but which lacks the finishing touches to make it fit an actual problem.

With this flexibility in mind, some possible models or skeletons are illustrated in this chapter. These are only a small selection from the many conceivable frameworks, and their primary purpose is to illustrate the use of skeletons in common types of situations.

These skeletons come halfway between the vagueness of a general problem-solving scheme and the explicitness of, for example, a plan for locating a specific factory in a specific place. They are designed to be approximately what is required for particular problem types and are based on actual experiences. They can next be elaborated or modified to fit the actual circumstances in which they will be used.

After using the strategy-building technique for awhile, certain favorite routines, or mini-strategies, will turn up, and these, too, can be incorporated as building blocks in full-size strategies. Such mini-strategies often contain sprinklings of questions from all over—some general, some quite specific. It is a good idea to build up a few of these, as they will be custom-made by ourselves for areas which are relevant and important to us. Thus we can rely upon them as genuine short-cuts of considerable value. However, we should still thoughtfully review their structure from time to time. Once any strategy has been built and used, its basic form can serve as a model to be used in later similar problems in just the way that the skeletons presented here are to be used.

So whether the user starts from the skeletons in this chapter, or from skeletons built up from experience in relevant situations, a core collection of models is a useful addition to the strategy-building process.

In living systems dynamic order is important. Things are organized, but flexibly so. Similarly, in the use of strategies, although we may have fairly fixed segments in our strategies, these must be used in an aware and flexible manner. There must be a readiness to modify an approach in the face of change or new perceptions. The gratifying feeling of pressing on with a predesigned plan, undaunted by adversity, can be misleading. The trick is to develop the wisdom to be able to distinguish when to stand firm from when to change direction quickly.

REMARKS ON USING SKELETONS

Before tackling the details of using skeletons, it is advisable to bear in mind some general remarks. In all strategies it is important to remember to choose the appropriate level of detail at which to operate. We penetrate different levels of our hierarchically constructed problem-solving plan, depending upon the requirements of the situation. In some cases we may wish to merely skim through a strategy at the section-title or strategy element description level, taking a very broad and cursory view. In some cases we may be working question by question through a strategy element group. It may also be that in different parts of the same problem we may need differing levels of effort.

If we overcomplicate our approach we may well become more confused than before. Or we may mistakenly convince ourselves that since we are expending so much effort we must be doing something worthwhile. On the other hand, skimping and cutting corners can lead to even more problems later. Hitting the right balance, streamlining our approach for maximum speed, and yet maintaining both inventiveness and thoroughness is a skill which requires practice.

As mentioned in the first chapter, a useful approach is to skim through the strategy, first applying it lightly in a generalized way to get the feel of the situation. Then, as we begin to get a picture of the principal areas of our problem, we can go through the strategy again at a more detailed level. If necessary, this could be done progressively until we feel confident that we have the right speed and depth.

If we are doing our weekly grocery shopping we clearly do not have the complex logistical problems of railroading, trucking routes and capacities, storage and distribution, and so on, that we would have if we were feeding an army. So why overdo it? After all, our purpose is to solve problems, not to devise elaborate strategies.

Although it may only take an hour or so to put together a fairly comprehensive strategy, the time taken for its execution will vary considerably. In the example given in the preceding chapter, the strategy could be worked through in a weekend, or it might occupy odd moments for a number of weeks or months. Some of the better ideas mature slowly after considerable effort and many false starts.

In cycling through these strategies, and also during cycles, it is advantageous, even essential, to let periods of intense activity alternate with relaxed meandering. New ideas, new syntheses, new possibilities of organization are more likely to occur during or after these relaxed periods than during a storm of detail. Continuous application can result in sterility, aridity, and uninspired solutions which do not contribute greatly to solving the problem.

GENERAL PROCEDURE FOR USING SKELETONS

In the next section we will be looking at the skeletons themselves. Let us now look at the general procedure for the use of these skeletons.

Selecting a Skeleton

As there are only four skeletons given here, selection is not much of a problem. We just need to give a little thought to the kind of area in which we are operating, and how we might try to deal with it. Then a glance at each skeleton and its prefatory remarks should be sufficient for selection. The four skeletons given here are fairly distinct, but as you collect a set of your own models, overlapping skeletons may require more thoughtful selection.

Modifying a Skeleton

Next we read through our chosen strategy skeleton and consider how it compares with the action that might be required in our situation. It may fit our situation fairly nicely as it stands, especially if we select our level of detail and specific questions with care. However, there may be a difference of emphasis in our project. We may wish to reorganize a skeleton into different groupings, with different, more appropriate labels and step descriptions. There may be steps we wish to leave out or add in—for example, we could include project teams, or we could add specific techniques or processes, and so on.

Employing a Skeleton

After we have selected and, if required, modified the skeleton most appropriate to our situation, we are ready to put it into action.

We can, if we choose, take a first run through the problem by using just the step descriptions and strategy elements included in the skeleton. This first time around we would not need to include the descriptions included under Level 2, where these secondary levels are marked in a skeleton. This preliminary approach will prepare us for dealing with the problem by starting the questions and difficulties floating around in our minds. This helps to give us a global view of the situation. It should also counteract any tendency for us to seize upon one aspect of the problem which then obscures our vision of the broader perspective. Unless we are dealing with a fairly small problem or an urgent, chaotic situation, we will not implement any solutions at this point as there has not yet been time to do anything properly.

After our initial survey of the problem we are in a position to advance to the next stage. Here we run through the skeleton a second time. Now we select actual question groups from the strategy elements whose full details are to be found in Chapter 7. The familiarity with the problem which we gained earlier will aid us in selecting the question groups. Once we have chosen our question groups, we can return to work on our problem using appropriate questions from the chosen groupings. Imagination will help in using the strategy questions to generate further questions more specific to our situation. We should take the time to answer our questions thoughtfully. We must try to avoid impatience because we are laying groundwork that will support later effort—especially if the first solutions arrived at are found to be flawed and we have to rethink everything.

On this second run-through we may well have been able to deal with our problem satisfactorily, especially if it was a small one*. For larger, more difficult problems or for fast-moving situations which require repeated efforts to close in on a solution, we need to go further. We may want to modify the skeleton at this point, to include further cycles or levels of detail if this seems fitting. Alternatively, we may now want to start another run-through at the next level of detail. In both cases we would now look at the problem with greater thoroughness and consider wider implications and deeper issues. As this will require a greater investment of time and effort we must be sure that our particular problem merits such effort. We do not need $2000 solutions to $20 problems. Assuming the problem merits further attention, we can now begin again concentrating on areas of particular difficulty which our previous efforts should have isolated.

By now we may want to modify our strategy somewhat as we gain a clearer perception of the problem. However we must beware of continually changing tactics in a frantic and disoriented effort to find a solution which eludes us.

*In the case of small problems we may have preferred to use the mini-strategy associated with each skeleton—see below.

In the following sections there appear four skeletons:

1. Diagnosis or problem definition.

2. Getting organized.

3. New ideas.

4. Entrepreneurial.

Accompanying each skeleton is a mini-strategy, a short and sharp miniature version of a complete strategy which might grow from the fully developed skeleton. These are rearranged slightly and retitled to fit their size. There is an exception in the case of the entrepreneurial skeleton, where the mini-strategy is a crisis strategy, something to put into effect immediately if a venture has run into serious difficulty.

The mini-strategies are designed for use with smaller problems and in relatively uncomplicated situations. They can also be used as starter strategies to get our bearings before a more comprehensive attack on a larger problem.

THE SKELETONS

DIAGNOSIS OR PROBLEM DEFINITION SKELETON

When trying to pin down complex and elusive causes of difficulties, defining nebulous problems, and clarifying issues, it is often hard to know where or how to start. To aid us in approaching such difficulties it is useful to reflect upon the diagnostic procedures of the medical world.

In medical diagnosis the physician is interested in moving from *how* the patient's problem is expressed to *what* the patient's problem is. Many different diseases have a large number of symptoms in common, so great care is required to ensure that the correct treatment is prescribed. Since the treatment is quite specific to the disease, treating the wrong disease may have alarming consequences.

Thus a clear perception of the problem is vital to the physician. Indeed a whole branch of diagnosis, differential diagnosis, deals with the art of clearly distinguishing one disease from another. This task becomes particularly elusive when dealing with interactions from more than one cause, and where disorders may be obscured or over-

laid by other symptoms. This may especially be the case in neuro-psychological problems, where the patient may accidentally or deliber-ately present misleading reports of symptoms. All this calls for great care and imagination on the part of the physician. Astute detective work is a critical part of medical practice.

In many other kinds of problems, however, we do not approach problem definition with anything like the same care or imagination. This lack of imagination is an important factor in poor problem defini-tion. The best medical diagnostician is one who sees interrelation-ships that no one else sees. This, of course, requires a creative and flexible approach. Such thinking is equally applicable to problem definition in other areas. A liberal addition of imagination to the definition stage would contribute greatly to avoiding something we see too often—great zeal in solving the wrong problem.

The same principles characterize medical diagnosis and problem definition—careful, painstaking analysis of imaginatively gathered data, and imaginative examination of painstakingly constructed con-clusions.

The following diagnosis or problem definition skeleton can be extended to philosophical or ideological difficulties where the data gathered might consist of views held by conflicting proponents and/or examples and implications of proposed postures. This is a popular method of philosophical analysis, in which a series of examples of the implications of a philosophical problem are examined for their paradoxical or puzzling nature, or their truth or falsity. Skill and imagination in gathering critical examples and perceiving awkward implications are among the distinguishing features of this kind of philosopher. Such principles are readily extended to pondering day to day political issues.

The need to use imaginative effort to break out of unduly constraining perspectives is just as important in our daily media-assailed life as in avoiding hoary philosophical cliches. Imagination is important not only to the physician and the philosopher but to all of us, as we make our way through the increasingly intermeshed and complex issues of modern life.

The strategy skeleton attempts to balance imagination and judgment. It further attempts to help us ride the thin line between open-minded collection of data and random accumulation of irrelevant facts, and between astute selection of highly probable swift routes to a likely solution and pedestrian, conventional habits of thinking. We must try not to repeat the mistake of the medical student who thinks that diagnosis begins with shrewd guesses and ends by attempting to bring the facts into line with the guesses.

As this skeleton covers a wide range of strategy elements, be sure to select questions sparingly. Otherwise your strategy will rapidly grow to unmanageable proportions.

THE SKELETON

Try using the following when attempting to pin down complex and elusive causes, for defining nebulous problems and clarifying issues.

1. What is the initial appearance of the difficulty?

What triggered the cry of "Problem," or is it just a suspicion? What does the situation look like? If it is "obvious," beware of being trapped by preconceptions. Make question selections from strategy element 1:

1–1. Initial assessment (1).

2.   Set initial objectives and standards for preliminary data gathering

Either form some initial hypothesis as to what might be going on, or form some idea as to the best areas to expend effort in finding this out. Open-mindedness is not quite the same as random data gathering. Make question selections from strategy elements 2 and 7.

2–1. Set project or solution objectives. (2).

2–2. Set standards and success criteria (7).

3.   Gather preliminary information

Quickly gather all available information, bearing in mind that you can save time by looking for evidence which contradicts your idea of what is happening. Information you gather may keep altering your perception of the problem. Do not let this disorganize you. Record your hypotheses and the pros and cons for each. Make question selections from the following elements:

3–1. Basic fact finding (11).

3–2. Available knowledge review (12).

3–3. Look at the history of the situation (13).

4.   Consider what the problem might be

Sift through the information you now have. Try to eliminate misconceptions or prejudices. Look for inconsistencies and areas where further information is needed. Now try to form a definite idea of what the problem is. Construct one or more clearly laid out hypotheses. Select questions from the following elements:

4–1. Examine overall structure or system (20).

4–2. Build model of situation (29).

4–3. Fact questioning and assessment (21).

4–4. Question assumptions (8).

4–5. Synthesize (26).

5. Plan data gathering for testing hypotheses

Think what is needed to make a good case for your hypothesis. How will you work out all the implications and make sure you have supporting data? Once your diagnosis is firm you will need to consider what could refute it. What loopholes are there? How could it be totally or partially misconceived? How will you decide? What extra information do you need? How can you get it? Select questions from the following elements:

5—1. Plan organization of operation (3).

5—2. Select appropriate techniques (4).

5—3. Devise appropriate tests (9).

Level 2. (Used if this turns into a larger scale operation).

5—4. Set up project team (5).

5—5. Set standards and success criteria (7).

5—6. Prepare implementation plans (33).

6.   Gather more extensive information

With a clearer idea of where to look and why, start a more thorough and detailed information hunt. Do not waste time with superfluous corroboration. Look for any information which might contradict your hypotheses. You will want to look also at how your information fits together and relates to larger matters. Select from the following elements:

6—1. Examine parts and interrelationships (16).

6—2. Look at neighboring systems (17).

6—3. Examine overall structure or system (20).

6—4. Project into the future (6).

Level 2.

6—5. Determine objectives implicit in the situation (14).

6—6. Determine information and decision making structures (15).

6—7. Assess system needs; resource consumption (18).

6—8. Assess demands upon the system (19).

7.   Reassess tentative diagnosis

Now that you are more or less overwhelmed by information relating to your hypotheses, it is vital to let all this filter quietly through your mind. Consider the possibility that there is an entirely different way to see all this. What new viewpoint could you take that would show all this in a different light? Pick at inconsistencies, paradoxes, and sneaking suspicions. What is *really* at work here? Select questions from the following elements:

7−1. Initial assessment of solution (30).

7−2. Build model of situation (29).

7−3. Determine implications and ramifications (31).

7−4. Question assumptions (8).

7−5. Assess approach so far (10).

7−6. Fact questioning and assessment (21).

8.   Attempt improved diagnosis

By now you should have a fair idea of what you think is happening. Pull it all together. Extract the best possible diagnosis. Form a clear definition of the situation before you, and thus set the stage for thinking out what to do about it. See if you can find any holes in your ideas. Try to improve them anyhow. Attempt to rethink and gain new perspectives. Select questions from the following elements:

8−1. Attempt improvement (32).

8−2. Take a different approach (23).

8−3. Juggle, juxtapose, and fantasize (25).

8−4. Synthesize (26).

8−5. Develop ideas into solutions. (27).

9.   Next step?

- If step 8 suggests any new lines of thought, return to step 5.
- If in step 7 or 8 the original hypothesis collapses, return to step 4.
- If everything is fine, review progress:

9−1. Assess merits and defects of this strategy (38).

(End.)

MINI-STRATEGY FOR DIAGNOSIS OR PROBLEM DEFINITION

Get Oriented

Make an initial assessment of the situation. Give consideration to what you are going to try to do, and why.

1−1. What are you trying to do?

1−1−8. What issues are you trying to resolve?

1−2. What kind of problem does this seem to be? Is it emotional, political, organizational, theoretical, financial, psychological, medical, or other; or what blend of various factors?

1−3−7. Which seem to be the critical areas?

1−5. At what level should the problem best be approached?

1−7. What is to be done?

Dig for Facts

Carefully look for information which will help you piece together what is happening.

11−5. What is happening? What difficulties are there, and what opportunities?

11−5−2. Where is it happening?

11−5−3. When is it happening?

11−5−4. How is it happening?

11−2−1. What areas are there?

11−2−4. What areas need the most effort, the most time, the most watching, the most thought?

11−6. What are the major variables and decision sequences?

11−6−6. Is there anything, any relationship, value, structural framework, process, or pattern which remains the same over any significant period of time?

12−1−1. What do you already know? What information is immediately available?

12−1−2. What has been said about, done about, written about it?

13−1−1. How were the present relationships or arrangements of events brought about? How did things get to be this way?

Reflect upon What You Have

Give thought to your information. Construct and examine some initial hypotheses as to what all this is about.

20−1−6. Can you see any decisive patterns at all?

20−2−7. What are the objectives of this framework, structure, or system?

21−1. Why do you perceive this to be a problem?

21−1−2. Is there anything that you know, any facts or information, which could show that what is seen to be the problem really is not?

21−2. Are you sure you have all the information you need?

21−2−2. Have your "facts" been corroborated by additional sources or means?

21−3−5. How many different interpretations can you think of?

21−4−1. What is connected to what? Can you draw a map or picture of your main facts? How is each one connected, or how should it be, to the others? Are there any missing connections?

21−4−2. Are there any interesting coincidences?

21−5−2. What have you missed?

8−1−4. What unquestioned assumptions have you made about, for example, the environment, political aspects, personal factors, technological aspects, the future, present trends, economic aspects, skills, training, policy, organization, and so on?

8−1−5. What value systems, beliefs, or attitudes are you assuming to be implicit in this situation? Are these assumptions valid? Could this change? What would be the effects?

8−2−5. Could someone be misleading you deliberately?

What Can Be Made of All This?

Now select a final diagnosis or problem statement. Is this hypothesis really tenable?

6−1. What might happen next? In the short term? In the long term?

6−1−3. Is there some reason why the future in this situation may differ considerably from the past?

6−1−6. How are the future developments likely to affect this system?

22−3−7. What else could be constructed from this?

23−1−1. Who could give you another viewpoint on this situation?

23−1−6. If you had an entirely different occupation, how might this problem look to you?

23−2−9. How can you modify the boundaries of this problem? Make it extend further, or not so far?

23−2−2. Can you change the viewpoint from which the problem is perceived, e.g., emotional, rational, personal, organizational, political, ethical?

24−2−4. What similar problems have you come across?

25−3−5. Look out your window. Think how the very first thing you see could be made to relate to the problem.

Pull It All Together

Explore the implications of your chosen diagnosis and tie up all the loose ends.

26−1−3. What are the bits and pieces you think are relevant?

26−1−4. What seem to be the key characteristics of this situation? What are the critical points?

26−1−5. How do you think these things might fit together? Have you a provisional, preliminary feeling for how all this goes together?

26−1−9. Is there some unifying principle you can invent, or borrow from somewhere else?

26−2. What concept will synthesize all this? Some old idea? Or must it be something new?

26−2−7. Are you using any idea, concept, viewpoint, metaphor, or synthesis in the most effective way?

26−3−9. Does this synthesis, viewpoint, or metaphor just lead to explanations of the current situation, or does it predict, generate new hypotheses, produce fruitful new avenues for exploration?

30−1−4. Has this been thoroughly thought through?

30−1−5. Does it form a coherent whole, does it hang together properly?

30−1−7. Are there any loose ends? If so, why?

30−2−1. Are you looking at the situation from too limited a perspective?

30−4−6. What other ideas are there, or have there been, which draw the opposite or very different conclusions from your idea?

30−4−7. What do you make of that?

30−4−9. Has your idea solved the problem, shifted it, or disguised it?

30−3−8. Are you afraid to throw it all out and start again?

GETTING-ORGANIZED SKELETON

Whether we are setting out to solve a large problem, managing by objectives, mounting a sales campaign, or launching a military offensive, we will falter unless we have organized ourselves effectively. Many good ideas collapse when implemented, and many well-intentioned efforts never get started through lack of organization.

Good organization requires forethought, a knowledge of where we are trying to go, and a grasp of practical realities. Organization is an interaction between the theoretical and the actual, and once again demands a balance of skills. We may carefully think out a way of carrying three loaded bags of groceries. However, practical reality may present us with the problem of negotiating a revolving door and

walking through the rain with our paper bags. Organizing effectively resembles the many-moves-ahead thinking of the chess player or military tactician. In our case the opponent is that jolly army of Murphy's Men with their monkey wrenches who are ever plotting the most ingenious ambushes.

The organizing facet of our activity does not allow itself to be bundled into the beginning of a project, labelled "Getting Organized," and then be forgotten. We must not only *get* organized; we must *stay* organized. This watch-dog organizing is a form of vigilance which we must carry with us at all times. Because the world is built upon fluctuating probabilities rather than certainties, we must constantly be prepared to resist disorganization, or to reorganize our efforts in advance of predicted difficulties. Once again imagination and practical judgment interweave to match courses of action to a series of possible scenarios.

At the same time, getting organized and staying organized do not mean that we have to have made all the decisions and solved all the problems before we act. When we are organizing we gain a perception of our task in the framework of the larger environment, issues, values, and objectives into which it fits and identify the decision areas, problems areas, and possible techniques and time frames, and we piece all these together into a viable action plan. We try to construct a course of action, an organization of effort, which will have the best results in terms of a coordinated progression towards our goal.

The accompanying skeleton offers a generalized strategy of organizing for action. It can be used alone or in conjunction with more involved techniques of systems analysis, operations research, or project management. In the latter cases its role might be that of a supervisor or overall monitor for any change of direction—scheduled or otherwise.

THE SKELETON

1. What are you attempting to achieve?

Getting organized is the detailed elaboration and implementation of a clearly conceived course of action. Unless this course of action *is* clearly conceived, implementation will be confused and hit-or-miss, and characterized by restarts, overruns, and, quite possibly, failure. It is vital to be precise in stating objectives at this stage. Select questions from the following elements:

1–1. Initial assessment (1).

1–2. Question assumptions (8).

1–3. Set project or solution objectives (2).

Level 2

1–4. Determine objectives implicit in the situation (14).

1–5. Fact questioning and assessment (21).

2. How well do you hope to do it?

Not only does what you intend to do have to be clearly outlined, but how well you expect to do it. Unless performance standards are clearly delineated it is hard to know how well you are doing until it is too late to correct any discrepancies. Select questions from the following elements:

2−1. Set standards and success criteria (7).

Level 2

2−2. Devise appropriate tests (9).

3. What do you already know?

Look at both the knowledge and experience you have, or can obtain about this situation, and what other people may have done. Although your situation may be unique, it is highly unlikely that somebody else has not done something resembling this. Learn from their experiences. It saves time and may avert failure. Select questions from the following elements:

3−1. Available knowledge review (12). (Concerning ways of handling projects like this).

3−2. Basic fact finding (11).

3−3. Look at the history of the situation (13).

Level 2

3−4. Project into the future (6).

3−5. Examine overall structure or system (20).

4. Initial structuring of effort and snag prediction

Having gained a clearer picture of the situation which you are going to tackle, it is now time to look to tactics. Where might effort be best directed? Try to predict obstacles, snags, breakdowns, and disasters. Consider alternate maneuvers to reach your objectives, and/or consider alternate targets. If one fails, try to be in a favorable position to start for the other. Examine the situation more closely, as required. Perhaps this particular operation is amenable to a special kind of technique appropriate to a particular profession, approach, or time. Perhaps a technique could be borrowed from somewhere else? See how time and effort might be reduced by an effective technique or techniques. Select questions from the following elements:

4−1. Plan organization of operation (3).

4−2. Look for similar situations (24).

4—3. Select appropriate techniques (4).

4—4. Devise appropriate tests (9).

Level 2

4—5. Set up project team (5).

4—6. Determine information and decision-making structures (15).

4—7. Look at neighboring systems (17).

4—8. Determine implications and ramifications (31).

5. Tie it all together

Now that you have the how, why, who, and what, put in the where, when, and in that order. Tie the project together into a scheme of plans and alternate plans with dates, deadlines, standards, measures, and so on. Select questions from the following elements:

5—1. Examine overall structure or system (of how your project fits into the context of the situation) (20).

5—2. Synthesize (26).

5—3. Build model of situation (29).

5—4. Prepare implementation plans (33).

Level 2

5—5. Question assumptions (8).

5—6. Fact questioning and assessment (21).

5—7. Take a different approach (23).

5—8. Juggle, juxtapose, and fantasize (25).

6. Attempt improvement of the plan

A first attempt on the plan makes us thoroughly familiar with what is required, but it is a rare first attempt that cannot be improved upon. The results of a second look should be well worth the time spent thinking it over. Improve it. Select questions from the following elements:

6—1. Initial assessment of solution (30).

6–2. Assess approach so far (10).

6–3. Attempt improvement (32).

Level 2.

6–4. Fact questioning and assessment (21).

6–5. Question assumptions (8).

6–6. Project the solution into the future (34).

7. Implement

Try it.

8. Keep it moving

Do not relax now. You may lose your grasp on the situation. Monitor, review, and pick out the potential problems, and solve them. If things threaten to get out of hand, quickly employ this strategy, or the mini-strategy, again in this step. Select questions from elements 10 and 3.

8–1. Assess approach so far (10).

8–2. Plan organization of operation (3).

9. Assess results

Whatever happened you can learn something for next time. Think it all over carefully and realistically. Select questions from elements 37 and 38.

9–1. Check results of solution (37).

9–2. Assess merits and defects of this strategy (38).

MINI-STRATEGY FOR GETTING ORGANIZED

Where and Why?

State in clear and precise terms exactly what it is you are trying to achieve.

2−1. What is your general objective?

2−1−2. What are your short term aims?

2−2. What are your specific objectives?

2−2−1. What are the specific characteristics of the situation you wish to bring about?

2−2−2. What will be the criteria for success? How will you decide when the problem is satisfactorily solved or your goal reached?

2−2−7. What is the least you *must* do?

2−2−8. What is the most you *can* do?

2−2−9. How soon do you want it done?

2−3−6. Do you have alternate goals? If you cannot achieve one, would another be satisfactory?

What Is the Situation?

Where are you starting from? What difficulties are you facing?

20−1. What is the overall situation?

20−1−2. Can a main focus of difficulty be isolated?

20−1−3. Can the situation be resolved into some fairly distinct categories, groups, or areas of difficulty?

20−1−4. Can the problem be broken into sub-problems which can fairly safely be dealt with separately?

20−1−8. Is there a principal focus of organization or control, a principal trouble spot or weak spot?

20−1−10. What characteristics are peculiar to the total situation? What does the whole have that the parts do not?

20−2. Where does this problem fit in the general scheme of things?

20−2−1. Is this part of a larger system or problem, and closely connected to it?

20−2−2. What assumptions are you making about the larger system, the background against which this situation is happening? Are they valid?

What Does Your Your Plan Have To Cover?

Where are you going to have to direct your attention?

3−1. As a result of the objectives, where might effort best be directed?

2−3−7. How many different paths might lead to your objective? Are some more appealing, more effective, more motivating, more fruitful, more economical, faster, less troublesome than others?

3−1−1. What areas are there?

3−1−2. Do they all have to be covered at this point?

3−1−3. Can they all be covered? If not, which merit the most effort at this point, or which arrangements of fragments are the most appropriate?

3−1−4. Which areas need the most effort, the most time, the most watching, the most thought?

3−1−5. Which have important sequencing or timing constraints?

3−1−6. Which activities are the most flexible, the easiest to accommodate?

3−1−7. Which activities are the most subject to uncertainty?

3−1−8. Which activities will have the greatest impact if they are delayed, fail, succeed?

26−1−4. What seem to be the key characteristics of this situation? What are the critical points? What is the crux of the matter?

3−2−4. Are there any basic, fundamentally important activities?

How Will You Do It?

What arrangement of activities will you have to initiate to deal with all this?

26−2−6. Is there some unifying principle you can invent or borrow from somewhere else?

3−2. How should effort be organized?

3−2−1. What sequence of actions is required? What timing is required?

3−2−2. How must the different tasks be organized to permit them to be achieved? Can it be done?

3−2−5. How long will each action take? If this is not known, how will it affect the way things fit together?

3−2−6. What alternatives are there in the event of failure along the way to each target?

3−4−3. What target dates, target amounts, or target positions are there?

3−4−4. What are the timing and target priorities?

33−1−7. Is a pilot scheme or some kind of trial run called for?

33−3−4. How long will implementation take? Who will be involved? Can they do it?

33−4−3. In the event of being able to accomplish only a part of your objectives, what are your priorities?

33−4−11. How might you make up for lost time or lost progress, if this is required?

3−6. What is the extent and what limitations are there to this project?

3−6−1. What is to be done?

3−6−2. When is it to be done?

3−6−3. What are the time dimensions?

3−6−4. Where is it to be done?

3−6−5. How is it to be done?

SKELETON FOR NEW IDEAS

Almost all of the creativity, idea generation, or scientific problem-solving approaches that have been devised include some method of twisting around or turning everything upside down. Popular creativity techniques use deliberate devices to turn thoughts into new channels. The attempt is usually made to juxtapose two incongruous planes of thought. Ideas "short-circuit" from one plane to the other and can present us with a new viewpoint or concept.

We have to break down old patterns and rebuild with new ones. We have to find a new direction, to restructure events in a novel form. We move from what we know into the unknown, and try to use this to extend what we know. The skeleton presented here is built upon this cycle of destructuring and restructuring.

The traditional explanation of creativity—consisting of fact-gathering, perspiration, incubation, and illumination—identifies the incubation period as its turning-about time. This may occur during daydreams, or in thinking about something else. The hypothesis is that subconsciously various twists and turns and rearrangements take place, and suddenly there it is—a reformulation of the situation which

might constitute a new idea. The trick now is to try to arrange our problem-solving activity to facilitate these basic processes.

We can see these creative principles reflected in the description that was given by "Cicero" in 1977, of progress so far in the iceberg-towing problem. The French consulting company mentioned in the Introduction started with the problem of towing very large icebergs. Initial study of the situation led them to narrow their ideas to a more specific objective: how to tow an iceberg about ¾ mile long, 900 feet wide and 900 feet high. This would produce approximately 10 million tons of water, or one billion liters. Further thought determined that it would take five or six tugboats six or eight months to tow it at one knot—which was considered to be the optimum speed. However, this meant that approximately 50 percent of the berg would melt during this period. It would need to be protected. How? Many creative ideas start from seemingly nonsensical origins. "Cicero's" next idea certainly appeared to fall into the structure-breaking category of nonsense. The idea? Put the iceberg into a tank of fresh water to protect it. Clearly this was asking the impossible. So how did they propose to turn the impossible into the possible? They thought of making an artificial lake on top of the iceberg to evaporate. The sides could be covered with metallic reflecting materials and the bottom wrapped in plastic. This still leaves problems unsolved—how to apply ¾ mile of plastic beneath an iceberg—but the path back from the ridiculous to the sublime begins to appear.

Implications of revolutionary ideas also need considerable thought. What would be the impact on Antarctica, where the icebergs would be collected, and on Saudi Arabia, where they would be melted? The effect on the Antarctic of purloining 100 icebergs per year was felt to be nil, as tens of thousands of icebergs are calved every year. In Saudi Arabia the effects were more interesting. The impact of the parked icebergs on Jidda, now in a desert region, was seen as lowering the temperature some four or five degrees. Furthermore the iceberg might lower the 90−95% humidity by condensing some of the water vapor in the air. Does this problem raise any strange or novel thoughts in your mind?

In the skeleton given here, we start with the structures that we have, the things we already know, familiar situations. We juggle this around, contort and twist it to get rid of the familiar structure. Under the guidance of the objective which the invention is to serve, we try to pull out a new pattern. Ideas of one kind or another will emerge to be tested. Then we can go back into the cycle until we come up with something really worthwhile. This skeleton must be handled with a light touch. It is not to be ploughed through ponderously. If ideas pop into our minds while we are working on some other part of the strategy we must note them. We follow them up if they tempt us. Then we can return and carry on. We don't stop ideas once they start to flow. The rest of the strategy can wait—but must not be *forgotten* about. Move quickly. Select questions with care and economy. Allow time for reflection, as it takes a little time to get the idea flowing. Furthermore, repeated sessions on different days will often allow us to approach the generation of ideas from new perspectives.

THE SKELETON

I.   Goals and Expectations

1.   What seems to be required?

Get your bearings. Give thought to where you think you should be exploring, and to what purpose. Make a selection of questions from the following strategy elements:

1−1. Initial assessment (1).

1−2. Set project or solution objectives (2).

2.   What seems to be involved?

Take a first look at the content and context of the situation. What kinds of things are happening or required? Select questions from the following:

2−1. Basic fact finding (11).

2−2. Available knowledge review (12).

2−3. Look at the history of the situation (13).

3.   Pin down objectives.

You may now have a clearer idea of the general form you are seeking. Try to formulate this with a little more clarity. Select questions from the following:

3−1. Question assumptions (8).

3−2. Set project or solution objectives (2).

3−3. Synthesize (26).

Level 2

3−4. Set standards and success criteria (7).

3−5. Plan organization of operation (3).

3−6. Select appropriate techniques (4).

II.   Idea Generation

4.   Explore more

Look for more information in general, and for more information along specific avenues provoked by your first perceptions of the situation. Try for a diversity of information to provide a fertile field for ideas. The purpose of this section is twofold. Firstly, it provides more information and a wider perspective. Secondly, it is meant to provide a mental loosening up, preparatory to a relaxed search for new ideas. Select questions from the following:

4−1. Look at neighboring systems (17).

4−2. Examine overall structure or system (20).

4−3. Examine parts and interrelationships (16).

4−4. Determine objectives implicit, hidden, or imbedded in the situation (14).

Level 2

4−5. Determine information and decision-making structures (15).

4−6. Assess system needs, resource consumption (18).

4−7. Assess demands upon the system (20).

5.   Try to formulate ideas

Try to think of a really original approach. Get away from the immediate confines of the problem. Look for something appealing, even startling. Go for real originality. Select questions from the following:

5−1. Take a different approach (23).

5−2. Fact questioning and assessment (21).

5−3. Juggle, juxtapose, and fantasize (25).

5−4. Synthesize (26).

Level 2

5−5. Question assumptions (8).

5−6. Assess approach so far (10).

5−7. Rearrange to provoke ideas (22).

5−8. Look for similar situations (24).

6.   Develop concept

If no concept has been synthesized at this point, return to step 4 or step 5. Even if one good idea has turned up, return to 5 or 4 for some more. *Only* when you have a number of alternatives, proceed through this step to step 7. In the present step any ideas are elaborated into solutions with at least some implementation planning. Select questions from the following:

6−1. Develop ideas into solutions (27).

6−2. Build model of the situation (29).

6−3. Determine implications and ramifications (31).

6−4. Attempt improvement (32).

Level 2

6−5. Devise information and decision-making structures (28).

III.   Assessment and Elaboration

7.   Start critical assessment

If you are taken with a fantastic idea, it is tempting to rush off in all directions and implement it. To prevent disaster, exercise restraint and look at your solution(s) with a critical eye. Assess ideas. Select best alternative if any. Otherwise return to step 5 or step 4. Select questions from the following:

7−1. Initial assessment of solution (30).

7−2. Assess approach so far (10).

7−3. Question assumptions (8).

7−4. Project the solution into the future (34).

Level 2

7−5. Assess energy and contribution of solution (35).

7−6. Assess impact and weaknesses of solution(36).

8.   Detailed elaboration

This is a small problem-solving sequence in its own right. The chosen idea is elaborated and any further research required is done as the situation is reexamined in light of the new concept. Detailed implementation plans should be developed at this point. The purpose is to turn ideas for solutions into real, full-size solutions. Avoid vague, ill-thought-out concepts whose only merit is a superficial appeal. Select questions sparingly from the strategy element groups below. If in a hurry just use Phase III.

Phase I. Research

8–1. Basic fact finding (11).

8–2. Available knowledge review (12).

8–3. Look at the history of the situation (13).

8–4. Examine parts and interrelationships (16).

8–5. Look at neighboring systems (17).

Phase II. Imaginative thinking

8–6. Examine overall structure or system (20).

8–7. Fact questioning and assessment (21).

8–8. Take a different approach (23).

8–9. Juggle, juxtapose, and fantasize (25).

Phase III. Elaboration

8–10. Develop ideas into solutions (27).

8–11. Devise information and decision-making routes (28).

8–12. Build model of situation (29).

8–13. Determine implications and ramifications (31).

8–14. Attempt improvement (32).

8–15. Prepare implementation plans (33).

8–16. Synthesize (26).

9. Final review

If critical difficulties are unearthed in this step, return to step 8, or even to step 5 or step 4. Select questions from the following:

9–1. Fact questioning and assessment (21).

9–2. Determine implications and ramifications (31).

9–3. Devise appropriate tests (9).

IV. Implementation and Assessment

10. Implement

Set the wheels in motion.

11. Assess results

What happened to your new idea? Why? What does this tell you about your idea, your performance, and the context in which it is taking place? What do you have to do now? Select questions from the following:

11−1. Check results of solution (37).

11−2. Initial assessment of solution (30).

11−3. Fact questioning and assessment (21).

11−4. Assess merits and defects of this strategy (38).

Level 2

11−5. Assess energy and contribution of solution (35).

11−6. Assess impact and weaknesses of solution (36).

11−7. Assess approach so far (10).

12. Next step?

If your solution is inadequate, return to step 1 or step 5 or 4.

MINI-STRATEGY FOR A NEW IDEA

What Seems To Be Required?

Review the problem you are trying to resolve and the goal you are aiming for.

1−1. What are you trying to do?

1−3−7. What seem to be the critical areas?

2−2−1. What are the specific characteristics of the situation you are trying to bring about?

8−1. Can you be certain that the problem is what it seems to be? Are you sure that *this* is the real problem?

8−1−4. What unquestioned assumptions have you made about, for example, the environment, political aspects, personal factors, technological aspects, the future, present trends, economic aspects, skills, training, policy, organization, and so on?

Explore the Situation

As a prelude to thinking about this problem in new ways, start to examine assumptions about this situation and its context.

8−1−5. What value system(s), beliefs, or attitudes are you assuming to be implicit in this situation? Are these assumptions valid? Could this change? What would be the effects?

11−1−3. What are the components of this problem? How many are there?

11−1−4. What are the attributes or characteristics of these components?

12−1−4. Is there a parallel that can be drawn from the past?

13−1−1. How were the present relationships or arrangements of events brought about? How did things get to be this way?

14−1−2. What really motivates activity in this situation?

17−2−3. What new arrangement of larger systems could make this problem disappear?

20−1−2. Can a main focus of difficulty be isolated?

20−1−4. Can the problem situation be broken down into sub-problems which can fairly safely be dealt with separately?

20−1−10. What characteristics are peculiar to the total situation? What does the whole have that the parts do not?

Twist and Turn and Generate Something New—*First Try*

Break your problem into pieces. Look at its different aspects separately. Play imaginatively with the bits.

21−2−9. What emotional blockages may be involved—in yourself or in others?

21−3−5. How many different interpretations can you think of?

21−4−2. Are there any interesting coincidences?

21−5−3. Is there any way of clarifying or making more specific the data which are available?

8−3. How can you make it all look different?

8−3−7. Can you change the level at which you are looking at this? For example, if you have to invent a new agricultural tractor would it help instead to think of new types of cultivation, or, alternatively, of new types of motive power or drive systems? So, can you take a wider view or more specific views?

22−1−1. Try grouping the parts of your situation according to their importance or relevance. What does this tell you?

22−1−2. Produce a checklist of specific characteristics required for your solution. Weight these for importance, cost, potential, and so on. Where does this point you?

22−1−3. Split the problem into its main aspects or dimensions and list the elements of each aspect or dimension. Then try looking at the actual, potential, possible, and remotely conceivable interactions of all those elements with each other, one by one. What do you find that you did not expect?

22−1−4. List all the attributes or functions of each component of your problem. Consider each attribute singly for its possible contribution. Change attributes to see what the effects might be.

Second Try

Start from somewhere else. Take a different approach. Go off on a tangent.

23−1−1. Is there a different way of describing your objectives? Perhaps a different statement, different angle, or viewpoint, will lead to different ideas for solutions.

23−1−6. If you had an entirely different occupation, how might this problem look to you?

23−2. What is the most prominent, captivating, stimulating, or useful-seeming aspect of this? Can you use it to find a new perspective?

23−2−11. Can you clear away any confusing, irrelevant debris? Can the situation easily be made less fuzzy?

23−3−9. What does it look like backwards? Can you turn the situation upside down?

24−1. What could be borrowed from somewhere else?

24−2−7. Have you come across similar situations in entirely different areas of your experience?

Third Try

How would you like to try something crazy? Insane ideas are often good stepping stones to sensible and practical results. Try it.

24−2−2. Can you find anything to spark off ideas in, for example, your kitchen drawers, office drawers, a department store, your toolbox, a supermarket?

25−1−6. How can different parts interact differently?

25−3. How could you solve this problem in a fantasy world? Why might this solution be made to work in the real world?

25−3−10. What is the most ridiculous solution you can think of? What is the craziest thing you could do?—that could happen? If you were put in charge of making this work sensibly, how would you do it?

26−1−5. What seems to be the most fruitful or rewarding direction for this to move in? In what areas are ideas or explanations for this most likely to be found?

Fourth Try

Concentrate on patterns. Start to formulate the beginnings of some real workable solutions.

26−1−4. What seem to be the key characteristics of this situation? What are the critical points? What is the crux of the matter?

20−1−6. Can you see any decisive patterns at all?

26−1−7. How can you pull all this together? What means can you use to grasp it all clearly?

26−2−6. Is there some unifying principle you can invent, or borrow from somewhere else?

26−3−2. Is there some way you can make all this seem more concrete, easier to handle?

27−1−1. How many different principles and processes seem to be involved?

27−1−4. What has to be balanced against what else? What pieces have to be made to interlock?

27−1−5. What parts could assist or support one another if acting together? Can this be arranged?

Examine Any New Ideas

Continue to develop your ideas imaginatively into workable solutions as you introduce a little critical assessment of what you have done.

30−1−4. Has this been thoroughly thought through?

30−1−5. Does it form a coherent whole? Does it hang together properly?

30−1−7. Are there any loose ends? If so, why?

30−3−3. Has this been thoroughly researched?

30−3−8. Are you afraid to throw it all out and start again?

30−4−9. Has your idea solved the problem, or shifted or disguised it?

34−1. Will this idea work in the future?

34−1−1. How are future developments likely to affect this system?

34−1−6. Imagine a disaster for your solution. How would you avoid it?

34−1−10. What would happen if the problem situation doubled itself, stopped, reversed, or increased tenfold?

34−2−6. Can you think of any reasons why your solution might make things worse?

SKELETON FOR AN ENTREPRENEURIAL SITUATION

The entrepreneur is working at a growing edge of society where diversity, innovation, and false starts proliferate. The entrepreneur, or entrepreneurial manager, operates in a hectic world of innovation and change. He or she interacts with a fast-moving environment in an atmosphere of risk and uncertainty and with fluctuating ground rules. The entrepreneur maximizes opportunities, producing diversity and opportunities for growth and energy production.

Considering a skeleton for an entrepreneurial strategy, it quickly becomes clear that the scope of problem management is wide, and a function of the total personality. To solve problems on the entrepreneurial front we do not merely have to examine a situation, tease out the real structure, and have enlightened ideas, we also need to have enormous energy, resiliance, determination, resourcefulness, to be highly alert to potential new opportunities and be able to redeploy, diversify, expand, or contract, as the situation or the shape of the future indicate.

The entrepreneur needs to locate his or her potential new venture in a fluctuating spectrum of factors including need, marketability, investment requirements, returns, competition, and social, technological, environmental and many other factors. This requires sensitivity in responding to clues as to the changing future of these factors and a quick appreciation of their real and potential interac-

tions. Aiming at ambiguous targets in the future means being prepared for risk-taking and conflict.

Because of this, initiated activity, responses, information seeking, and so on, must be similarly fast moving, and yet embracing awareness and contingency-planning in the face of risk.

So, in preparing a strategy which may act as a guide for an entrepreneur, we need to look principally at the posture adopted for information and opportunity seeking, invention, and sensitivity to the environment and its future. The skeleton introduced below is intended to help in feeling our way with a new idea, or in search of a new idea or opportunity into a future of uncertainty, while attempting to maximize the use of available feedback.

It might be said that the entrepreneur is the last person who should be constrained by a strategy. To an extent this is true. However, even guerrilla warfare is fought with a general plan and under specific tactical guidelines. With objectives clearly in mind, relevant opportunities are more readily identified. With attention paid specifically to the value and reliability of information actively sought, the shape of the future wherein the opportunities lie can be seen a little more clearly. With a practised skill in innovating, opportunities can be more reliably provoked, and adversity more easily turned to advantage. The use of strategies is intended to contribute to these abilities. At the same time, the use of the attached skeleton will have to be fast and vigorous. No time is available for ponderous cogitation.

THE SKELETON

1.   Get the feel of the situation.

Find out what you have to learn, whom you need to contact, what kinds of things are available, possible, likely, or unlikely, and compare this with your initial ideas. This is an idea-generating, opportunity-perceiving interaction between the environment and your basic goals.

1−1.   **Adopting an initial stance.** Analyse your objectives, look at the overall situation, and adopt an initial orientation to the challenges perceived. Select questions sparingly from the following elements:

1−1−1.   Set project or solution objectives (2).

1−1−2. Question assumptions (8).

1−1−3. Basic fact finding (11).

1−1−4. Project into the future (6).

1−1−5. Examine overall structure or system (20).

1−1−6. Set standards and success criteria (7).

Level 2

1−1−7. Select appropriate techniques (4).

1−1−8. Devise appropriate tests (9).

1−1−9. Plan organization of operation (3).

1−2. Pinpoint targets. Make a more specific analysis of the situation and pinpoint target areas. Select questions sparingly from the following elements:

1−2−1. Available knowledge review (12).

1−2−2. Look at history of the situation (13).

1−2−3. Project into the future (6).

1−2−4. Examine overall structure or system (20).

1−2−5. Fact questioning and assessment (21).

1−2−6. Synthesize (26).

Level 2

1−2−7. Determine information and decision-making structures (15).

1−2−8. Examine parts and interrelationships (16).

1−2−9. Look at neighboring systems (17).

1−2−10. Assess system needs, resource consumption (18).

1−2−11. Assess demands upon the system (19).

1−3. Generate target attainment ideas. Develop ideas for achieving the goals set or targets selected.

1−3−1. Rearrange to provoke ideas (22).

Level 2

1−3−2. Take a different approach (23).

1−3−3. Look for similar situations (24).

1−3−4. Juggle, juxtapose, and fantasize (25).

1−4. **Develop target attainment plans.** Turn the ideas into action plans for achieving your goals.

1−4−1. Synthesize (26).

1−4−2. Develop ideas into solutions (27).

1−4−3. Plan coordination of operation (3).

1−4−4. Prepare implementation plans (33).

Level 2

1−4−5. Build model of situation (29).

1−4−6. Devise information and decision-making routes (28).

2.   Draw up more specific plans

for implementing ideas generated or for taking advantage of opportunities perceived, and put out feelers to test or estimate their feasibility. Expand your information collection and assessment and dissemination system to achieve this and to maintain awareness of the ever changing scene.

2−1. **Assess plans.** Critically assess the plans made, attempt to improve them, and, if not already done, develop contingency plans for potential difficulties.

2−1−1. Assess approach so far (10).

2−1−2. Initial assessment of the solution (30).

2−1−3. Project the solution into the future (34).

2−1−4. Question assumptions (8).

2−1−5. Attempt improvement (32).

2−1−6. Fact questioning and assessment (21).

2−1−7. Plan organization of operation (3).

2−1−8. Prepare implementation plans (33).

Level 2

2−1−9. Determine implications and ramifications (31).

2−1−10. Build model of situation (29).

2-1-11. Assess energy and contribution of solution (35).

2-1-12. Assess impact and weaknesses of solution (36).

2-2. Develop measures of success. Work out what your measures of success will be and turn these into specific standards and progress measures.

2-2-1. Set standards and success criteria (7).

Level 2

2-2-2. Select appropriate techniques (4).

2-2-3. Devise appropriate tests (9).

2-2-4. Plan organization of operation (3).

2-2-5. Set up project team (5).

2-3. Take another look. Once again look over the situation for any new developments. Reexamine specific situations and local conditions. Reassess targets and contingency plans and attempt improvement.

2-3-1. Basic fact finding (11).

2-3-2. Project into the future (6).

2-3-3. Available knowledge review (12).

2-3-4. Fact questioning and assessment (21).

2-3-5. Assess approach so far (10).

2-3-6. Initial assessment of solution (30).

2-3-7. Project the solution into the future (34).

Level 2

2-3-8. Look at the history of the situation (13).

2-3-9. Determine information and decision-making structures (15).

2-3-10. Examine parts and interrelationships (16).

2-3-11. Look at neighboring systems (17).

2-3-12. Assess system needs, resource consumption (18).

2-3-13. Assess demands upon the system (19).

2-3-14. Determine implication and ramifications (31).

2-3-15. Assess energy and contribution of solution (35).

2-3-16. Assess impact and weaknesses of solution (36).

Act

Carve out your niche, consolidate, increase the speed and effectiveness of your information and response systems, watch the situation, be prepared to exploit any breakthrough, look for new opportunities. Then go back to step 1, as new situations arise through ideas generated or opportunities perceived, and as the competition brings out new ideas to counteract you.

3–1. **Action.** Act on target plan, using progress measures and watching developments closely.

3–1–1. Assess approach so far (10).

3–2. **Review.** Review results and reconsider objectives, as required.

3–2–1. Check results of solution (37).

3–2–2. Initial assessment of solution (30).

3–2–3. Assess approach so far (10).

3–2–4. Set project or solution objectives (2).

3–2–5. Assess merits and defects of this strategy (38).

3–3. **Reassess.** Reassess overall situation for new opportunities or dangers.

3–3–1. Basic fact finding (11).

3–3–2. Project into the future (6).

3–3–3. Available knowledge review (12).

3–3–4. Examine overall structure or system (20).

Level 2

3–3–5. Look at history of situation (13).

3–3–6. Determine information and decision-making structures (15).

3–3–7. Examine parts and interrelationships (16).

3–3–8. Look at neighboring systems (17).

3–3–9. Assess system needs, resource consumption (18).

3–3–10. Assess demands upon system (19).

MINI-STRATEGY FOR A CRISIS

Although this is intended for use at times of crisis, it is advisable also to use it for contingency planning in advance in an imaginative consideration of possible future crises.

In a crisis one of the first priorities is to maintain or restore morale and a will to solve the problem. Often a first response is a dazed disorganization and a tendency to negative recriminations or resigned apathy. The use of this mini-strategy is intended to direct thinking during this problematic phase. It is also intended to make possible the thought that the crisis may even be a blessing in disguise. The guerrilla fighter operates in a turbulent world of rapidly shifting circumstances and, by definition, against an enemy who is better equipped, better fed, and often better trained. In such situations crisis is the rule rather than the exception. One of the prime requirements of the guerrilla is to be able rapidly to turn a bad situation to his or her advantage. So, like the guerrilla, the entrepreneur—and the rest of us too—must take a positive approach to difficulty and try to twist it to advantage. A large part of the accompanying mini-strategy is devoted to looking for new opportunities offered by disaster. In this way we try to introduce not only a little order into a turbulent situation, but also a little optimism.

1. What *must* be rescued, protected?

Act to guarantee survival of basic functions and purposes.

2−1−1. Do you have clear exactly what it is you are trying to achieve?

23−2−11. Can you clear away confusing, irrelevant debris?

3−1−1. What areas are there?

3−2−4. Are there any basic, fundamentally important areas?

3−1−3. Can they all be covered? If not, which merit the most effort at this point, or which arrangements of fragments are the most important?

3−1−8. Which activities will have the greatest impact if they are delayed, fail, succeed?

2−2−7. What is the least you *must* do?

2−2−8. What is the most you *can* do?

6−1. What might happen next?

10−5. What have you missed?

2. How might this be done?

Get organized—and fast—and get into action!

1−4−4. How fast are things happening?

1−3−7. What seem to be the critical areas?

3−2. How should effort be organized?

3−2−1. What sequence of actions is required? What timing is required?

3−2−9. Are there any activities which could suddenly become vital? Is there enough flexibility to allow these to be accommodated?

3−3−1. What has to be done to push this through fast?

3−4−7. What will you do in case of emergency? How will you organize yourself? What will you have ready to put into action?

12−2−3. Who can help you with this?

10−1−3. Is enough being done?

10−3−6. Can effort be reduced in any area?

3. What new opportunities does this catastrophe offer?

Despite the apparent disaster, does this situation still offer some opportunity to turn everything to your advantage?

2−3−3. How can you turn your troubles to your advantage?

8−1. Can you be certain that the problem is what it seems to be? Are you sure that *this* is the real problem?

21−4−2. Are there any interesting coincidences?

17−2−3. What new arrangement of larger systems could make this problem disappear?

21−3−6. Is there, or could there be, some other explanation of this?

24−1−6. Is some part of this process similar to any other process?

22−2−7. What else could be constructed from this?

23−1−9. How can you sneak up on this problem? What indirect approach can you take? What unexpected angles could you try?

23−3−9. What does it look like backwards? Can you turn the situation upside down?

25−3−8. Can you see the humorous side of this? How could you make a joke, using parts of this problem? How could you use it?

Chapter 5

A Complete Strategy

This chapter contains the fully developed version of the "What should I do?" life-style strategy that was assembled in Chapter 3. Its principal purpose is to illustrate how a complete strategy might look.

This strategy is designed for a leisurely, meditative approach to the problem of finding a new direction for life to take. It is a rather long strategy with a considerable number of questions to contemplate. As this represents an ambitious attack upon the problem, haste in its execution would be disadvantageous.

With a little imaginative adaptation this strategy could be modified to answer the question of "What should our company do?"

In the first four steps additional material has been included. This consists of elaborations of the strategy element questions. These are more specific to the particular situation than the generalized strategy element questions. They illustrate how strategy element questions can be used to trigger thinking in a given situation. These extra questions follow each strategy element question. The strategy element questions appear on separate lines and the numbers in the text are the numbers of the strategy element questions in Chapter 7.

The purpose of the apparent repetition in this strategy is to ensure that you take a second look at various areas after you have thought through them once, and perhaps gathered further information that might allow you to take a different perspective. As your knowledge of a problem grows, so does the possibility that you can change your relationship to it or your involvement with it. This process, if con-

116

sciously pursued, should allow you to reach out for more imaginative and competent solutions to your difficulties.

You may wish to try changing some of the questions for others that you find more personally stimulating or fruitful.

THE STRATEGY

1. Find your Good Points, Potential, Talents

Think hard to discover your good points. Use some imagination, brainstorm, remember, ask other people. You may surprise yourself. Everyone has some strong point. Look at what you have done and what you have enjoyed in the past.

STRATEGY ELEMENT 11: BASIC FACT FINDING

11−1−1. What is the overall situation?

What do you consider to be some of the more important things in life? What do you get the most enjoyment out of doing, being, feeling, responding to? What do you find rewarding, uplifting, worthwhile?

11−1−2. What are the major trends? What are some of the minor trends? What forecasts have been made?

Where do you seem to function well? Where do you seem to function less well? What direction do these qualities seem to be taking? What do other people think you could do well?

11−1−3. What are the components of this problem? How many are there?

In how many areas do you function well? What skills. what attitudes, what personal qualities do you do well with? What talents and what potential do you think you have?

11−1−4. What are the attributes or characteristics of these components?

Go into some detail looking at these good points. How are they good? Why are they good?

11−1−5. What are the most significant, important, or urgent aspects of this problem? Why?

What seem to be your most significant good points? Which are the most valuable to you yourself, to your friends, to the world around you?

11−4. What is being done? What action is being taken?

In what circumstances do your good points appear? In your daily life, where, when and how do you accomplish things you feel pleased with? Why does this happen?

11−4−1. Why is it being done?

11−4−2. How is it being done?

11−5. What is happening? What difficulties are there and what opportunities?

In what circumstances do good things happen to you? How do these come about?

11−5−1. Why is it happening?

11−5−2. Where is it happening?

11−5−3. When is it happening?

11−6. What are the major variables and decision sequences?

Now look more closely at all this. Look for patterns, look at attitudes. See how it all fits together. Perhaps you may see your good points in a new light. Perhaps you will discover potential good points or good qualities you overlooked.

11−6−2. What attitudes are involved?

11−6−4. What values are involved?

11−6−6. Is there anything, any relationship, value, structural framework, process, or pattern that remains the same over any significant period of time?

11−6−7. What elements or aspects are involved in any pattern you see?

11−6−10. What and where are the strong points?

11−6−11. What have you missed?

Don't you have a few more good points than this? Think a little harder for some of the points you are so used to that you don't even notice them any more. What does anyone else think?

STRATEGY ELEMENT 13: LOOK AT THE HISTORY OF THE SITUATION

13−1. Has it always been like this?

What is the history of your good points? What have you achieved or what have you been like personally? What has hindered the development of your good points?

13−1−1. How were the present relationships or arrangements of events brought about? How did things get to be this way?

How have your good points developed? How have they changed with time?

13−2. What is the history of the system that contains this problem?

How are your good qualities related to life around you? How have people responded to you? What events have transpired?

13−2−2. What seem to be the significant events, trends, personages, and influences involved?

What has been going on in life around you in relation to your good points?

13−2−6. Will attempts to deal with this difficulty turn out to be a waste of time when the historical path of the situation is considered?

Take care not to swim against the tide. Get straight what your good points are as opposed to what you wish they were. Follow your greatest strengths.

13−2−8. Does consideration of the past highlight any potential future problems or developments?

Upon what solid foundation of good qualities could you start to build for the future?

2. How Could These Good Points Grow?

Think how your good points, or potential good points, might be developed. What could you turn them into? How could you become better at what you are good at?

STRATEGY ELEMENT 6: PROJECT INTO THE FUTURE

6–1. What might happen next?—in the short term?—in the long term?

Where do you think your potential will be used? How could you make it grow? In what circumstances will your talents flourish? In the next few weeks and months? In the next few years?

6–1–1. Is there some reason why the future of this situation may differ considerably from the past?

Are you at a time of great potential change? Are things changing around a lot? Are there a great number of unknowns?

6–1–2. Can you figure out what will replace the present situation and its solution?

Does the future of your good qualities seem to have a definite shape? If not, how could you make one? How could you encourage their growth? Through a particular career, profession, location, life-style, partner?

6–1–3. When might events in other areas alter the shape of this problem?

Keep your eyes open. New laws, new social developments, crises on the horizon, and other possibilities, might change everything, bringing opportunity or adversity.

6–2–4. Are you looking far enough ahead?

If it's a question of life-style, you need to consider today, tomorrow, and 20 years from now in some form or other.

STRATEGY ELEMENT 25: JUGGLE, JUXTAPOSE, AND FANTASIZE

25–3. How could you solve this problem in a fantasy world? Why might this solution be made to work in the real world?

What could you grow into or turn yourself into? A giant, Einstein, Michelangelo, a saint? What would your fantasy world look like? How would you fit into it? What would you spend your time doing? How would other people feel about you and respond to you? What does this tell you?

25–3–2. If you were a frog, how would you perceive this problem? How would it be different? Why?

If you were a frog you would be well adapted to life in ponds. You could leap around with strong legs, swim powerfully, breathe on land, and yet stay under water. You'd have big eyes to detect movements—flies to eat, pike and ducks to avoid. How can you adapt yourself to your world as well as the frog has done? What constitutes your equivalent of powerful swimming legs, of ponds and reeds, pike and ducks? How could you be a better frog?

25–3–4. If one of the people involved in this were a porpoise, how would things have to change?

If your spouse, daughter, best friend, boss, employee, or father turned into a porpoise, what would you have to do? Which of your good qualities would be strained? What would be overtaxed? What does this tell you?

STRATEGY ELEMENT 24: LOOK FOR SIMILAR SITUATIONS

24–2–1. Can you think of any analogies from plant life, insect life, your garden or local park, the seashore, the zoo, the woods, the desert?

Are you like a spider spinning an overcomplicated web of life and getting caught in it? Are you a porpoise swimming freely, relying on skills rather than possessions or position? Are you like a lizard in the desert, expertly making use of minimal resources?

24–2–3. Are there any useful analogies to be found in electrical systems, mechanical systems, physiological systems, acoustical systems, weather systems, etc.?

Are your emotions as unpredictable as the weather? Can your good points all be made to support each other and act in concert, like the human body with its fine balance of breathing, heat-generating, shivering, heartbeat control, digestion, alarm systems, excitement, and so on?

24—2—4. Can you find anything comparable in history, in different social groups, cultures, civilizations?

Can you find a parallel for the role you wish to play? Are you a Caesar, a Napoleon, a Socrates, a Michelangelo, a Leonardo, a Galileo, a Joan of Arc, a Helen of Troy, a Machiavelli? How would you avoid the mistakes they made?

3. Where Would You Like To Go Ideally?

What would you like to do? What kind of situation do you wish to work toward? If you don't have any dreams, generate ideas based on your good points and/or any conceivable opportunities. Where do you want to go? How do you want to get there? Develop some ideal objectives.

STRATEGY ELEMENT 6: PROJECT INTO THE FUTURE

6—1. What might happen next?—in the short term?—in the long term?

What are your inclinations? What do you daydream or fantasize about? How would you like the future to take shape? What do you really want to become? What would you like to happen to you, or do, or experience in the next few weeks or months? What would fulfill your dreams? Where would you really like to be 10 years from now? Would you really? Think about it.

6—1—3. When might events in other areas alter the shape of this problem?

Do your ideals and dreams fluctuate and change shape with day to day events? If you set off on a course of action, would you keep changing direction and get nowhere? Or have you a more permanent dream or hope? If so, is there anything that could interfere with your achieving it?

STRATEGY ELEMENT 2: SET PROJECT OR SOLUTION OBJECTIVES

2−1−1. Do you have clear exactly what it is you are trying to achieve? What general state of affairs are you trying to bring about?

Can you achieve a clearer picture of what you would like to do? Can you get beyond the daydream stage to a more specific, detailed picture?

2−2−4. What degree of success are you aiming for?

Can you get there in stages? Do you have to go all the way? How far? How soon?

2−2−5. What degree of success will you be satisfied with?

What are your minimum requirements? What would feel rewarding?

2−2−6. Which will be the key characteristics of success? Which will be the less important characteristics?

What attributes are important to you? Can you pin down your priorities?

STRATEGY ELEMENT 25: JUGGLE, JUXTAPOSE AND FANTASIZE

25−1. Magnify the effect or characteristics of one part of your problem.

What if one of your talents were fully developed and expressed right now? What difference would this make to the situation? If you were a fully competent painter or administrator already, how would this affect your aspirations? Where do you really want to go?

25−1−1. Magnify the personal aspects.

What if the effects of your actions on your family were doubled, trebled? What if your personal resiliance were halved, doubled?

25–1–3. Change the impact of decisions made.

What if your choices affected a whole city or nation? What if they affected nobody? What if they affected a different set of people or events? What if their effects were more severe, more rewarding, more tedious, more fun?

25–1–9. Can you think of any way at all (think really hard) in which ideas for this situation could be sparked off by thinking about a button?—a candle?—a hinge?—a wheel?—a can?—a bush?—a meteor?—a caterpillar?—a gate?—the sun?—a river?—an explosion?

4. Imaginatively Reconcile the Ideal or Desirable with Your Good Points

How might you adapt what you would like to do to fit your good points in practice? Can you satisfy the objectives you have in a way that builds upon your strengths? If you don't seem to be able to achieve your dreams, is there something that might substitute? Perhaps you can arrive at some intermediate stage that might help you in a later new attempt at the ideal? Develop some personally realistic objectives.

Look for a New Viewpoint

In this section the task is to twist and turn to gain different viewpoints or insights into the situation. Move everything around slightly, changing the value, degree, or extent of what you can do or what you want, and see what happens. You are searching in all directions for a way to get the best of both worlds by thinking up a really good idea to do what you want within your present limits. You are the only person who can figure this out. In the following, take one question at a time and concentrate on it. Let your ideas flow freely. Record them. Don't strike out the silly ideas until later. Use them to reach good ideas. Don't feel compelled to use more than a handful of the questions given.

STRATEGY ELEMENT 22: REARRANGE TO PROVOKE IDEAS

22–2. Change the size of one element of the problem.

22–2–7. Change the type of people involved.

22−3−1. Change the way in which one part of the situation is being done.

22−3−3. Change the speed at which one part of the situation is happening.

22−3−4. Eliminate one of the things that is happening.

22−3−6. Change around the location of the parts or events.

22−3−8. What would happen if the problem situation doubled itself, stopped, reversed, or increased tenfold?

22−3−9. Change the style of the whole operation.

STRATEGY ELEMENT 23: TAKE A DIFFERENT APPROACH

23−1−2. Who could give you another viewpoint on this situation?

23−1−10. How can you sneak up on this problem? What indirect approach can you take? What unexpected angles could you try?

23−2. What is the most prominent, or captivating, or stimulating, or useful-seeming aspect of this? Can you use it to find a new perspective?

23−2−2. Can you change the viewpoint from which the problem is perceived, e.g.: emotional; rational; personal; organizational; political; ethical?

23−2−3. Would any of the above viewpoints change your perception of the problem?—making it more simple, complex, understandable, or challenging?

STRATEGY ELEMENT 24: LOOK FOR SIMILAR SITUATIONS

24−1. What could be borrowed from somewhere else?

24−1−1. What other process is similar to this?

24−1−2. What else has a configuration like this?

24−1−3. Who else does something like this?

24−1−4. What else functions like this?

24−2. What analogies or metaphors for this situation can you find?

24−2−5. What similar problems have you come across?

STRATEGY ELEMENT 25: JUGGLE, JUXTAPOSE, AND FANTASIZE

25−1−5. Can you pull your situation to pieces like a jigsaw puzzle, and then put it all back together in various different ways?

25–3. How could you solve this problem in a fantasy world? Why might this solution be made to work in the real world?

25–3–5. Look out your window, and think how the very first thing you see could be made to relate to the problem.

25–3–9. What is the most ridiculous solution you can think of? If you were put in charge of making the solution work sensibly, how would you do it? What is the craziest thing you could do?—that could happen?

Give Your Insights Some Structure

Having explored a number of ideas, can you now pull it all together, make sense of it all, and settle on some realistic and practical objectives that still reflect your dreams?

STRATEGY ELEMENT 26: SYNTHESIZE

26–1. What are you trying to feel your way toward?

Can you produce some simply stated overall goal of a practical, realistic nature? Like: *self-development through an individual enterprise involving aerial photography;* or: *to make a maximally supportive contribution to agricultural research;* or *to generate the maximum joy and growth in my immediate family circle by . . .* , and so on.

26–1–2. What are you trying to construct?

Now elaborate your main goal. Give some details. Split it into sub-goals if necessary.

26–1–4. What seem to be the key characteristics of this situation? What are the critical points? What is the crux of the matter?

What are your top priority concerns? What are the most important constraints? What are going to be the recurrent themes, rewards, obstacles? Start to lay out the pieces.

26–1–6. How do you think these things might fit together? Have you a provisional, preliminary feeling for how this goes together?

Can you see the time frame involved? The expense? The effort required? A specific timetable? Chance factors? Deadlines?

26–2–8. Is it too soon to attempt such a synthesis?

Should you get more ideas first? More information? More experience? More advice? Think harder? Take a break? Have a change of scene?

STRATEGY ELEMENT 2: SET PROJECT OR SOLUTION OBJECTIVES

In section 3 you looked at ideal objectives. Now look again, but consider practical objectives for which you can devise implementation plans. Here you need to be specific.

2–2–1. What are the specific characteristics of the situation you are trying to bring about?

2–1–2. What are your short term aims?

2–1–3. What are your long term aims?

2–1–4. Are your objectives realistic? For yourself? For others involved?

2–1–6. What do your goals imply? What tasks do they lead to?—within what time frame?

What exactly will you have to do, and how well will you have to do it?

2–2–2. What will be the criteria for success? How will you decide when the problem is satisfactorily solved?—or your goal reached?

Vague objectives bring vague results. If you do not have clear objectives you will almost certainly get lost or lose interest later on. Even when you are trying to puzzle through a confusing situation, a statable objective will help negotiate the vagueness of the situation.

2–2–7. What is the least you *must* do?

2–2–8. What is the most you *can* do?

2–2–9. How soon do you want it done?

2–3. How can you gain the maximum contribution from solving this problem?

If you are going to all this trouble, make sure you get as much as possible out of it.

2–3–1. Are you sure this is what you really want?—or what is really needed?

If it is not, you will probably be faced with a series of restarts, and eventually you will become discouraged.

2–3–3. How can you turn any difficulties to your advantage? What new opportunities might there be? How might these be exploited?

This takes imagination, but sometimes tackling obstacles successfully brings pleasant surprises.

2–3–4. Have you detected and acknowledged your strengths and weaknesses—or those of others involved—and planned around them?

If you haven't they'll lie in wait for you.

2–3–5. In the event of only being able to accomplish a part of your objectives, what are your priorities?

Can your dreams take more than one shape? If one avenue is blocked can you open up another?

2–3–6. Do you have alternate goals? If you cannot achieve one, would another be satisfactory?

2–3–7. How many paths might lead to your objective? Are some more appealing, more effective. more motivating, more fruitful, more economical, faster, less troublesome than others?

2–3–8. How might they all compare? How might you select?

5.   Produce Realistic Plans

How might you put this into effect? What practical steps might you take to make your objectives attainable? Try to maintain a balance between aiming so high that you will be discouraged by complete failure, and aiming so low that you will not be challenged and your successes trivial and unrewarding. This is a mini-problem-solving effort in its own right.

STRATEGY ELEMENT 7: SET STANDARDS AND SUCCESS CRITERIA

7–1–1. What will be the key characteristics of success? What will be the less important characteristics?

7-2-7. What will you be weighing and assessing to determine a solution's acceptability?

STRATEGY ELEMENT 11: BASIC FACT FINDING

11-1-5. What are the most significant, important, or urgent aspects of this problem? Why?

This time look at this and the next few questions with respect to the difficulties that may face you in developing your good points, as well as the opportunities.

11-5. What is happening? What difficulties are there and what opportunities?

11-5-1. Why is it happening?

11-5-2. Where is it happening?

11-5-3. When is it happening?

11-5-4. How is it happening?

11-6. What are the major variables and decision sequences?

STRATEGY ELEMENT 12: AVAILABLE KNOWLEDGE REVIEW

12-1. What previous knowledge or experience can be called upon? Where can this be obtained?

12-1-1. What do you already know? What information is immediately available?

12-1-2. What experiences have other people had who have gone through this kind of thing? What did they learn? How can you find out?

STRATEGY ELEMENT 16: EXAMINE PARTS AND INTERRELATIONSHIPS

16-1. What relationship does each part have with each other part?

16-1-1. What is connected to what? Can you draw a map or picture of your main facts? How is each one connected, or should be, or could be, to the others? Are there any missing connections?

16-1-3. What specific influences are at work? Which of these might operate in your favor or in favor of the system's objectives?

16−1−4. What might be some of the long-term ramifications, influences and interrelationships?

STRATEGY ELEMENT 20: EXAMINE OVERALL STRUCTURE OR SYSTEM

20−1−2. Can a main focus of difficulty be isolated?

20−1−4. Can the problem be broken down into smaller parts which can fairly safely be dealt with separately?

20−2−2. What assumptions are you making about the larger system?—the background against which this situation is happening? Are they valid?

20−2−3. Should a larger encompassing problem be attacked?

STRATEGY ELEMENT 21: FACT QUESTIONING AND ASSESSMENT

21−1−7. Can you be certain the problem is what it seems to be? Are you sure *this* is the real problem?

21−1−9. Why is this not just one problem?

21−1−10. Do you feel you have really grasped what is happening?

21−1−11. Where does this problem fit in the general scheme of things?

21−2−8. What is there that you don't know or are unsure about?

21−5. Have you checked it, even though it might seem to be "obvious?"

21−5−2. What contradictions or inconsistencies can you see?

21−2−9. Who could give you another viewpoint on this situation?

21−3−9. What psychological blockages may be involved, in yourself or in others?

STRATEGY ELEMENT 8: QUESTION ASSUMPTIONS

8−1−3. What unwarranted assumptions are you making? Can you list *all* the assumptions you are making—especially those too obvious to question—and examine each one?

8−1−7. What value system(s), beliefs, or attitudes are you assuming to be implicit in this situation? Are these assumptions valid? Could this change? What would be the effects?

8−1−9. What are you refusing to acknowledge?

8−2−7. Is there anything you consistently overlook, or don't pay much attention to, or emphasize, or concentrate on when looking at problems? How is that affecting this situation?

8−3. How can you make it all look different?

STRATEGY ELEMENT 14: DETERMINE OBJECTIVES IMPLICIT, HIDDEN, OR IMBEDDED IN THE SITUATION

14−1−2. What really motivates activity in this situation?

14−1−9. Are the objectives appropriate to the situation?

14−2. What hidden or unstated objectives might there be?

14−2−2. Are the real objectives disguised by the expressed objectives?

14−2−7. Do stated objectives conflict with what is actually happening? If so, deliberately or accidentally?

STRATEGY ELEMENT 22: REARRANGE TO PROVOKE IDEAS

22−2−1. Change the shape of one element of the problem.

22−2−4. Change the value of one element of the problem.

STRATEGY ELEMENT 23: TAKE A DIFFERENT APPROACH

23−3. Why can't you change the overall system of which this is a part?

23−3−6. Reorganize around the problem. Avoid the problem. Isolate the problem.

23−3−9. What does it look like backwards? Can you turn the situation upside down?

23−3−10. What would happen if the problem situation doubled itself, stopped, reversed, or increased tenfold?

STRATEGY ELEMENT 24: LOOK FOR SIMILAR SITUATIONS

24−2−2. Can you find anything to spark off ideas in: your kitchen drawers, office drawers, a department store, your toolbox, a supermarket?

STRATEGY ELEMENT 25: JUGGLE, JUXTAPOSE AND FANTASIZE

25−3−1. If this took place on another planet, would the problem be significantly different?

25−3−7. If you had a magic wand and could change this situation, how would you do it?—and what does this tell you?

STRATEGY ELEMENT 26: SYNTHESIZE

26−1−5. What seems to be the most fruitful or rewarding direction for this to move in? In which areas are ideas or explanations most likely to be found?

26−1−3. What bits and pieces do you think are relevant?

26−2−5. Is there some way of achieving a simpler overview of this whole thing?

26−3−7. Can you chop it all up into broad groupings and then deal with the groupings separately, so as not to be overwhelmed by the details?

STRATEGY ELEMENT 3: PLAN ORGANIZATION OF OPERATION

3−1. As a result of the objectives where might effort best be directed?

3−1−4. Which areas need the most effort?—the most time?—the most watching?—the most thought?

3−1−5. Which activities have important sequencing or timing restraints?

3−1−7. Which activities are most subject to uncertainty?

3−1−8. Which activities will cause the greatest impact if they are delayed?—fail?—succeed?

3−2. How should effort be organized?

3−2−1. What sequence of actions is required? What timing is.required?

3−2−6. What alternatives are there in the event of failure along the way to each target?

3−2−8. What can be arranged to permit taking advantage of an unexpected opportunity or reversal?

STRATEGY ELEMENT 27: DEVELOP IDEAS INTO SOLUTIONS

27−1−4. What has to be balanced against what else? What pieces have to be made to interlock?

27–3–3. What are your alternate plans and priorities? What are your emergency plans?

STRATEGY ELEMENT 33: PREPARE IMPLEMENTATION PLANS

33–1–4. Should it be phased in gradually?

33–1–5. Is an interim solution demanded while a more thorough investigation is undertaken?

33–2–9. Do any other things need to happen to make your solution possible? If so, how are you going to ensure that they do?

33–1–7. Is a pilot scheme or some kind of trial run called for?

33–3. Is implementation properly planned and organized?

33–3–1. What steps and stages are required? What will you do if these get out of joint?

33–3–3. How will you time the implementation of your solution? When would be a good time? When would be a bad time?

33–4–1. How will you watch out for side effects or unanticipated future problems?

33–4–2. What will you do if things don't go according to plan?

33–4–7. What would happen if your solution failed completely? Have you a plan for that?

6. Assess Your Plans

How realistic, appropriate, and rewarding are your plans? Here you will want to avoid doing things that will fall foul of your weaker points. Make sure your plans have taken account of any of your less strong points.

STRATEGY ELEMENT 30: INITIAL ASSESSMENT OF SOLUTION

30–1. Is this doomed from the start?

30–1–3. Are you closing your eyes to anything?

30–1–4. What are the greatest risks? Where are the greatest challenges? Can these be handled?

30–1–5. Has this been thoroughly thought through?

30–1–8. Are there any loose ends? If so, why?

30−2. Don't you really need a broader outlook? Are you looking at the situation from too limited a perspective?

30−2−10. What contradictions or inconsistencies can you see?

30−3−4. Are the objectives of different parts of the solution, or the system into which the solution will fit, consistent? Do any objectives conflict with each other?

30−3−10. Are you afraid to throw it all out and start again?

STRATEGY ELEMENT 31: DETERMINE IMPLICATIONS AND RAMIFICATIONS

31−1−1. How does this problem compare and relate to other problems and events?

31−4. Have you analysed the various solutions with respect to any trade-offs which may have to be made?

31−4−1. If each of your solutions has a number of possible outcomes and you cannot decide which solution is best, can you decide which solution contains an outcome that would be worst?

31−4−3. Who grows, develops, benefits, as a result of this situation?

31−4−4. Who suffers as a result of this situation?

STRATEGY ELEMENT 16: EXAMINE PARTS AND INTERRELATIONSHIPS

16−2−6. When do parts get out of step?

16−3. Is this going to affect something else?

16−4. Do all these elements or parts form a coherent structure—that is, do all these interrelationships, or apparent interrelationships, make sense?—and does the whole thing make sense?

STRATEGY ELEMENT 34: PROJECT THE SOLUTION INTO THE FUTURE

34−1. Will this idea work in the future?

34−1−1. How are future developments likely to affect this system?

34−1−9. What if some unexpectedly beneficial future event occurs? Is there enough flexibility in your solution to permit you to gain maximum advantage from this?

34−2−3. Is there some reason why the future in this situation may differ considerably from the past?

34−2−6. Can you think of any reason why your solution might make things worse?

34−2−8. Are you looking far enough ahead?

STRATEGY ELEMENT 10: ASSESS APPROACH SO FAR

10−2. Is this the most effective way to do this? Is this the best action you could be taking?

10−2−4. Are you covering this in sufficient depth?

10−2−7. Is anything in jeopardy?

10−4. Do you need help or redirection?

10−4−1. Do you need a morale boost? Do you need improved resiliance? Can friends help?

10−4−2. Are you trying to do too much, or are you making rash responses to stress, or sudden uncontrolled change?

10−6−1. To what degree is this linked to, approaching, or on a collision course with anything else?

10−8. What are the strengths and weaknesses of this approach? What are you overlooking?

10−8−1. Are you working in areas of maximum contribution potential?

10−9−1. Have you planned as far as it is possible to plan, given the circumstances?

7. Are Your Plans Acceptable?

If acceptable, go to step 10. Otherwise, if any improvement could be made, carry on with step 8.

8. Attempt to build more rewarding, more fulfilling plans

Now that you have worked your way through your aspirations and difficulties to some kind of plan, sit back and think it over calmly and without pressure. Perhaps daydream a little. Can you now come up with something more appealing?

STRATEGY ELEMENT 32: ATTEMPT IMPROVEMENT

32−1. How can this be made more effective?

32−1−6. How can this be made more stimulating? How can this be made more motivating?

32−2−2. Can you pursue this in greater depth?—with greater energy?—with greater talent?

32−2−3. Does your solution apply to anything other than the immediate situation? Can you extend its principles to other areas?

32−2−4. Could it be blended with some other idea to produce something new?

32−2−5. Which is the best part? Can it be made better?

32−2−6. Which is the worst part? Can it be eliminated?

STRATEGY ELEMENT 23: TAKE A DIFFERENT APPROACH

23−1−2. Who could give you another viewpoint on this situation?

23−2. What is the most prominent, stimulating, captivating, or useful-seeming aspect of this? Can you use it to find a new perspective?

23−2−9. How can you modify the boundaries of this problem?—make it extend further?—not so far?

23−2−10. Can you focus on a weakness in your situation and turn it into an unexpected bonus?

STRATEGY ELEMENT 26: SYNTHESIZE

26−1−4. What seem to be the key characteristics of this situation? What are the critical points? What is the crux of the matter?

STRATEGY ELEMENT 27: DEVELOP IDEAS INTO SOLUTIONS

27−1−3. Do you have clear exactly what it is you are trying to achieve?

27−1−7. What new elements, possibilities, opportunities does your idea provide?—how?—where?—when?—why?—for whom?

27−1−10. Is there anything bothering you in this solution? Are you facing it, or covering it up?

27−4. In what directions can you best develop your idea?

27−4−2. Would it help to look around for further ideas, information, or analogies?

9. Assess any new plan

If any new plan or modification has appeared, go to step 6 for assessment.

10. Implement

Now start to put your plan into effect. Keep your eye on it. Watch closely to see if things are going according to plan and be ready to respond to any problems which may turn up. There are always teething troubles to be dealt with, so don't be upset when they appear.

STRATEGY ELEMENT 10: ASSESS APPROACH SO FAR

10−1. Are you making a genuine advance?

10−1−1. Are the activities underway adequate?

10−1−4. Is what is being done being done well enough?

10−1−7. Are the overall objectives being attained?

10−1−9. Can you minimize activities that do not contribute directly to overall objectives?

10−3. Are you keeping things moving and coordinated?

10−3−5. What rearrangement of activities or effort can be made to permit maximum progress? Is there anything that can be left, suspended, slowed down, to permit redirection of effort?

10−3−6. Can effort be reduced in any area?

10−10−1. Are you changing tactics too often? Are you losing your grip on the situation?

10−10−2. Are you managing to keep a clear picture of the parts of the situation? Can you detect uneven progress or the approach of trouble?

10−10−3. Do you need to do the same things but organize them better?

10−10−5. Have there been any surprises? If so, why?

10−10−9. Has your conception of the problem changed to the extent that your approach must change?

STRATEGY ELEMENT 3: PLAN ORGANIZATION OF OPERATION

3–3–3. How can separate parts or people support, motivate, or boost one another?

3–3–5. How can morale, resiliance, and enthusiasm be maintained?

3–3–6. Is massive, steady, or intermittent effort most appropriate?

11.   Assess the Outcome

Your plans may not have turned out exactly how you had hoped, or the situation may have altered drastically. You may now want to modify your plans, or you may just want to record your experiences for next time. Or you may want to start over.

STRATEGY ELEMENT 37: CHECK RESULTS OF SOLUTION

37–1. Did the solution work? If not, why did it fail? How long did it survive, and why?

37–1–1. If the solution failed, can it be patched up until a new one is ready?

37−1−3. If the solution failed, was it completely inadequate and out of touch with the reality of the situation?

37−1−4. If the solution failed, has it upset anything else, and if so what will you do about it?

37−1−5. Does the reason for failure present you with any insights?

37−2. If the solution was a success can it be improved?

37−3−1. Does the solution meet the requirements or objectives previously established?

37−3−2. What and where are the weak points?

37−3−3. What and where are the strong points?

37−3−5. What unforeseen problems arose and why?

37−3−7. Is the solution really working, or are appearances deceiving you?

37−3−8. Is the solution going to continue working like this, or is something going to go wrong sooner or later?

STRATEGY ELEMENT 38: ASSESS MERITS AND DEFECTS OF THIS STRATEGY

38−1. How well did the approach work?

38−1−1. What and where are the strong points? What do you think the good points about your approach have been—efficiency, speed, interest, enjoyment?

38−1−2. What and where are the weak points? What do you think the bad points about your approach have been—wrong direction, too cumbersome, disorganized, uninspired?

38−1−4. Look at the points where you didn't feel so sure of yourself? Why was this? Is it important? What can you do about it?

38−3. Was this the most effective way to do this? Was this the best action you could have taken?

38−3−1. Could you have done this faster? Could you have done it sooner?

38−3−2. Did you waste time anywhere?

38−3−4. Did you cover this in sufficient depth?

38−3−6. Did you dissipate your efforts? Could your work have been more concentrated?

38−4. How can you benefit from this situation for similar situations in the future?

38−5−3. Can you improve your problem-solving methods so that you can produce better solutions faster in the future?

12. Next step?

If you think you should start again, go to step 1. If you want to modify your plans, go to step 5. Otherwise this is the last point in the process—for now.

PART II

THE STRATEGY
ELEMENTS

In Chapter 6 are listed the strategy element names and their descriptions. This is where a first selection would be made.

In Chapter 7 is a full listing of questions associated with each strategy element. These questions are assembled into conveniently small groups. Each group usually covers a particular area of that strategy element.

There is also a separate index of the strategy elements grouped under the six phases of the problem-solving process. This should facilitate selection of strategy elements, since several can be used in more than one place in the process.

These strategy elements are not meant to be mutually exclusive. Some degree of overlap is unavoidable. Nor is it claimed that this breakdown is the only way to divide up the problem-solving process. The only claim is that this is a convenient and practical way to do it, and that this procedure reduces the difficulty of dealing with complex problems.

Each strategy element is marked according to the phase of problem solving with which it is associated. The abbreviations used are:

Plan (P)

Define or Diagnose (D)

Idea Generation (IG)

Solution Building (SB)

Solution Assessment (SA)
Approach Assessment (AA)

Following is an index of strategy element numbers listed under their appropriate problem-solving stages. The most applicable items are set in boldface.

Planning

1, 2, 3, 4, 5, **6,** 7, 8, 9, **10**

Diagnosing

4, 6, 8, 9, 10, **11, 12, 13, 14, 15, 16, 17, 18, 19, 20, 21,** 29

Idea Generation

4, 8, 10, **21, 22, 23, 24, 25,** 26

Solution Building

3, 4, 5, **7,** 8, 10, **16, 17, 18, 19, 20,** 26, 27, 28, 29, 31, 32, 33, 34

Solution Assessment

4, 8, 9, **10,** 11, 12, **21,** 22, 23, **30,** 31, **32,** 33, 34, 35, 36, 37

Approach Assessment

8, 10, 38

Chapter 6

Strategy Element Descriptions

The 38 strategy element descriptions that follow are the building blocks used to turn a rough skeleton into a basic strategy. This procedure is described in Chapter 3, page 43. In some cases problem solving can begin once these building blocks have been assembled. This is possible for small problems and for a first attack on larger problems. Usually it is preferable to follow these basic building blocks with a further breakdown to the level of strategy questions, as given in Chapter 7.

1. INITIAL ASSESSMENT (P)

Just what kind of situation do you have here? Try to establish in general what kind of difficulties you are faced with, and where it looks as though effort should be directed, and how. Get straight what seems to be going on, and you'll be in a better position to start tackling it.

2. SET PROJECT OR SOLUTION OBJECTIVES (P)

Clarify what you are trying to do in solving the problem. What are you trying to achieve and for what purpose? How far do you wish to go, and how will you know when you have succeeded? What are your priorities? What values are involved?

3. *PLAN ORGANIZATION OF OPERATION (P, SB)*

In nearly all problem-solving efforts there are people, materials, scheduling, sub-problems, activities, or all of these and more to arrange. This must be considered early, as it may be critical to the success or even feasibility of the venture. Figure out what the parts of the operation will be, and what comes where. Who does what and when? What needs to happen before what? What needs to happen in concert?

4. *SELECT APPROPRIATE TECHNIQUES (P, D, IG, SB, SA)*

There are different kinds of approaches, and these may need different tools or techniques. Select those which suit the problem. You may need imagination-boosting techniques, or forecasting tools, or means of personnel assessment. You may need precise, quantitative measures, or perhaps intuitive, qualitative means are called for. Try to get this clear and choose accordingly.

5. *SET UP PROJECT TEAM (P, SB)*

Where a team is required, get the right people for the job and arrange for them to work together harmoniously. Some people are imaginative but disorganized, some are resiliant and slogging but dull, some are good strategists and organizers but cannot cope with stress, some are great socializers but never have ideas. People are a mix of qualities. Don't put people where they won't work out.

6. *PROJECT INTO THE FUTURE (P, D)*

The present problem, and particularly the context in which it is set, is going to change. See what the future is likely to be in the short term and in the long term. Sometimes in this way a problem becomes less of a problem, or part of a bigger problem, or just looks entirely different.

7. *SET STANDARDS AND SUCCESS CRITERIA (P, SB)*

Both your approach to the problem and the kinds of solutions you propose must be of high quality. Set yourself standards and targets and measure yourself against these as you go. If you don't have some kind of standard and performance measure, you will have difficulty knowing whether you are on target, are going too slow or too fast. or are getting lost. Give yourself some kind of road map of expectations.

8.   QUESTION ASSUMPTIONS (P, D, IG, SB, SA, AA)

Unquestioned assumptions can play a large part in preventing you from seeing the crux of a problem, taking a viewpoint which would help you solve it, or seeing disastrous flaws in a solution. So you may often fix or eliminate a number of alternatives without even knowing it. Try to determine with which assumptions, ground rules, givens, dogma, style, principles, or theory you are approaching your problem, and see what might be revealed if you changed them. Does this open up any new avenues or offer any new insights? Are you blundering blindly?

9.   DEVISE APPROPRIATE TESTS (P, D, SA)

There are many times when you need to apply tests or measures in the course of problem solving. Not only is it necessary to have feedback on your progress and to test your ideas—as in strategy element 7—you also have to be able to determine what is actually going on in various complicated situations, whether something is or is not true or valid, whether a solution is likely to function in real life, and so on. How do you know what you claim to know? How do you find out and test it?

10.   ASSESS APPROACH SO FAR (P, D, IG, SB, SA, AA)

One of the difficulties of problem solving is that the whole situation can change its apparent shape as you get closer to it. In cases like this a completely different approach can be required. You must watch your progress carefully as well as watching the problem's shape. Has the situation taken on a different aspect? Do you need to reconstruct your approach? Are you doing less well or better than you had planned? What are you going to do about it? How can you adjust your efforts for greater effect?

11. BASIC FACT FINDING (D, SA)

The way you set about getting straight exactly what is going on can either blind you to the truth or help you get straight to the heart of the matter. You can flounder around, or you can quickly get the picture you need. You can also be misled as to whether you do have it all straight or not. If you don't get it right here you will only solve your problem by accident. Here you are setting the scene for more thorough analysis. Find out what's involved, who's involved, what's happening, how it's happening, why, where, and when.

12. AVAILABLE KNOWLEDGE REVIEW (D, SA)

Often the very problem you are dealing with, or something very similar, has been solved many times before. Find this out before you plunge into a full scale attack. If it has not, it is still helpful to find out if anything is known about similar situations. If you can get help from someone with experience or ideas in this direction, so much the better. Also make sure you know what you think you know. Check it out.

13. LOOK AT THE HISTORY OF THE SITUATION (D, SA)

Perspective and clues can be gained from finding out how long the problem has been going on, or what its origins are. Has it been gradual, sudden, intermittent, long-standing, recent? Problems sometimes look a lot different when you see how they grew. This may contribute to a knowledge of what might happen next.

14. DETERMINE OBJECTIVES IMPLICIT, HIDDEN, OR IMBEDDED IN THE SITUATION (D)

With what declared aims and intentions are participants in the situation acting? Do their actions reveal other objectives, multiple objectives, hidden objectives, or lack of objectives? What are the real purposes, intentions, or objectives involved in the situation? Often the real motivations for action are accidentally, unconsciously, or deliberately obscured. Some imagination may be required to unearth these.

15. DETERMINE INFORMATION AND DECISION-MAKING STRUCTURES (D)

It is critical to determine the web of communications which run through any human activity, as this plays a large part in who decides to do what, and why, and on the basis of what information. The form and adequacy of the messages and communications need to be established. The manner in which decisions are made, when, why, and how, also need to be known.

16. EXAMINE PARTS AND INTERRELATIONSHIPS (D, SB)

Many situations are very intricately interwoven structures where actions in one part may have startling results in other areas. Unless a clear picture is gained of what is connected to what else, it is quite likely that some unpleasant surprises will turn up when you try to take action. What is joined to what, why, and how?

17. LOOK AT NEIGHBORING SYSTEMS (D, SB)

Surrounding systems often play a large part in why a particular situation takes the form it does. Problems within a system may have external causes or external effects. No problem occurs in isolation. What effect is it having elsewhere? What else affects the problem situation? In what context is it set? Against what background is it taking place?

18. ASSESS SYSTEM NEEDS, RESOURCE CONSUMPTION (D, SB)

What does it take to keep this situation going? How much has to be done to keep it in operation? Is this appropriate? How? Why? Is everything in balance or not?

19. ASSESS DEMANDS UPON THE SYSTEM (D, SB)

What is the role of this system? What support does it provide? Where and why does it make its contribution? Who needs it, and for what? What would be the full implications of its disfunction?

20. EXAMINE OVERALL STRUCTURE OR SYSTEM (D, SB)

How does everything fit together? What is the total picture, what are the principal characteristics, what are the patterns and trends? Where is it all going? What whole do all the parts contribute to?

21. FACT QUESTIONING AND ASSESSMENT (D, IG, SA)

Now that you think you know all there is to know about the situation, or at least have all the critical information, what do you think is happening? Things are sometimes not what they appear to be. Don't get caught. Make sure your facts are facts. Look for oddities.

22. REARRANGE TO PROVOKE IDEAS (IG, SA)

Try pulling the situation around a little in your mind. Change pieces here and there and imagine what the effects might be. Does this provoke any new viewpoints or insights? Can you break out of fixed ways of looking at the situation?

23. TAKE A DIFFERENT APPROACH (IG, SA)

Sometimes, by going in a straight line, you may miss the answer. If you can find a way to approach the situation from an entirely different direction or in another frame of mind, you may see perspectives otherwise hidden.

24. LOOK FOR SIMILAR SITUATIONS (IG)

Analogies, metaphors, comparisons of all kinds are a prolific source of novel approaches. You can often borrow from elsewhere with startling results. Nature is a good place to start, since so many problems have been solved in ingenious ways in the natural world.

25. JUGGLE, JUXTAPOSE, AND FANTASIZE (IG)

Turn it all inside out and upside down. Resort to any or all kinds of fantasy, follow your nose, chase will-o-the-wisp ideas and see where

STRATEGY ELEMENT DESCRIPTIONS **149**

they might lead. Sometimes something eminently sensible turns up at the end of a trail of nonsense.

26. SYNTHESIZE (IG, SB)

Now try to pin down your new viewpoints or insights. Or try to pull together all the parts that are jumping around and make a unique pattern out of them. Try to simplify, unify, get a good grasp of what is required as a solution, and turn up a new synthesis.

27. DEVELOP IDEAS INTO SOLUTIONS (SB)

Perceiving a solution, having that bright idea, that masterstroke, is only the beginning. To convert a brilliant insight into a practical idea requires an investigation of what it will take to make it work. Work out the details and see where this leads.

28. DEVISE INFORMATION AND DECISION-MAKING ROUTES (SB)

Now you have to construct or adapt the web of information routes and the means of decision making so that your solution can actually operate and survive in the real world.

29. BUILD A MODEL OF THE SITUATION (D, SB)

Before rushing into action, see how far you can test your solution or diagnosis without actually implementing it. Construct a detailed model, picture, structure of some kind which will make plain the workings of your solution or situation. What happens?

30. INITIAL ASSESSMENT OF SOLUTION (SA)

Now is the time for rigorous criticism. Start to pick holes in your solution; ruthlessly hunt out the flaws. If you can pick any hole in it, you can be sure that life would have ripped it to shreds.

31. *DETERMINE IMPLICATIONS AND RAMIFICATIONS (SB, SA)*

Can you see how it is linked to various parts of the rest of the situation? Can you see what the implications are? Don't let the structures or dynamics of your idea remain vague. Spell out how it will operate, interact, or react in the various postures or stances it will be expected to take, or might unexpectedly be forced into.

32. *ATTEMPT IMPROVEMENT (SB, SA)*

You might be surprised at how much better you can make it. Don't stop at the first workable solution. Hunt out the good points and see if you can make them even more effective. Then go for the weak points and see if you can get rid of them.

33. *PREPARE IMPLEMENTATION PLANS (SB)*

Knowing what the solution is will not help if you cannot get it into operation. Don't fall on your face on the last lap. Having come so far it only makes sense to ensure that your work will not be wasted. Make sure it will appear in real life.

34. *PROJECT THE SOLUTION INTO THE FUTURE (SB, SA)*

Don't consider this solution only in the context of the present. Adopt a wider viewpoint. Your solution will take place in the future. Tomorrow will be different. Make sure it will fit. Don't give anybody a bad tomorrow.

35. *ASSESS ENERGY AND CONTRIBUTION OF THE SOLUTION (SA)*

What support will your solution give? What good things will it provide? Will the world really be a better place because of what you will have done? If not, why not?

36.   *ASSESS IMPACT AND WEAKNESSES OF SOLUTION (SA)*

Make a final rigorous hunt for the flaws in your solution and the detrimental effects they may have. It is still not too late to do it right. What have you missed?

37.   *CHECK RESULTS OF SOLUTION (SA)*

Well, what happened? What surprises were there and why? Can you still make improvements? Is there anything you have to put right? Keep watch on the situation; it may still surprise you. Are you sure your solution is working?

38.   *ASSESS MERITS AND DEFECTS OF THIS STRATEGY (AA)*

What do you think now of the approach you took on this problem? What have you learned from it? How will you act differently in future? Is there anything you did well which you can capitalize upon?

Chapter 7

Questions for Strategy Elements

Here the strategy elements described in the previous chapter are further subdivided. Each strategy element is broken down into groups of questions covering various aspects of that element. See Chapter 3, pages 53ff, for the way these questions are used to form a fully developed strategy.

1. INITIAL ASSESSMENT (P)

1-1. What are you trying to do?

1-1-1. What are your goals, objectives, or dreams here?

1-1-2. What do your goals imply? What tasks do they lead to and within what time frame?

1-1-3. In the event of being able to accomplish only some of your objectives, what are your priorities?

1-1-4. Can you be certain that the problem is what it seems to be? Are you sure that *this* is the real problem?

1-1-5. Is the problem too big for you alone?

1-1-6. What is there that you don't know, or are unsure of?

1-1-7. What is the penalty if you are wrong or fail?

1−1−8. What issues are you trying to resolve?

1−1−9. What puzzles you?

1−2.   What kind of problem does this seem to be? For example, is it emotional, political, organizational, theoretical, technical, financial, psychological, medical, or other; or what blend of various factors?

1−2−1. What principles are involved?

1−2−2. How complex does this problem seem to be? How many parts and levels does it seem to have?

1−2−3. Is this problem worth solving? If so, what degree of effort seems appropriate?

1−2−4. Where does this problem fit in the general scheme of things?

1−2−5. Is this part of a larger system or problem, and closely connected to it?

1−2−6. Should a larger encompassing problem be attacked?

1−2−7. What other systems, structures, or frameworks directly influence or are influenced by this system?

1−2−8. Is it primarily a matter of getting organized, of establishing priorities, of seeing where everything fits?

1−2−9. Is it a question of discovering information, assessing the truth of something, testing, or diagnosing?

1−2−10. Is it necessary to invent something new, to produce a new scheme or idea?

1−2−11. Is it a question of sorting out a muddled, distressing situation, avoiding some bad possibilities, or getting out of a bad situation?

1−3.   What seems to be happening? What difficulties are there, and what opportunities?

1−3−1. How long has it been going on?

1−3−2. What functions seem to be involved?

1−3−3. What attitudes are involved?

1−3−4. What values are involved?

1−3−5. How many people seem to be involved?

1-3-6. What legal, financial, psychological, or other requirements might there be?

1-3-7. What seem to be the critical areas?

1-4.   What special characteristics does this operation or situation have? What needs to be done to accommodate or take advantage of these?

1-4-1. How does this problem compare with and relate to other problems and events?

1-4-2. Can a main focus of difficulty be isolated?

1-4-3. Is there a principal focus of organization or control, or a principal trouble spot or weak point?

1-4-4. How fast are things happening?

1-4-5. If there is uncertainty in the situation, is it completely uncertain and completely unpredictable, is it uncertain with particular limits, or can some kind of probability be assigned to the situation?

1-4-6. How specific should you be? How much accuracy is necessary? How much effort will it take to be completely right, as opposed to nearly right? Is it worth it or needed? What is appropriate at this stage?

1-5.   At what level should this problem best be approached?

1-5-1. What style of operating, behavior, or approach is most appropriate to this phase of the problem-solving process or to this kind of problem?

1-5-2. What kind of approach suits the kind of uncertainty or complexity in this situation?

1-5-3. What priority for solution should this problem have?

1-5-4. Is an interim solution demanded while a thorough investigation is undertaken?

1-5-5. Can this problem be broken down into smaller parts which can fairly safely be dealt with separately?

1-5-6. If so, what needs to be borne in mind, what conditions need to be met, or what objectives have to be satisfied for the sub-problems to be dealt with separately and later pulled together for the total solution?

1−6.   How many different kinds of solution to this problem might there be?

1−6−1. How many different principles and processes seem to be involved?

1−6−2. What type of solution are you looking for here, e.g:

    a. An operational plan of some duration?

    b. An invention or new idea?

    c. A decision-making system or organizational structure?

    d. A conceptual structure or theory?

    e. A project plan?

    f. A search for specific information?

    g. Or, what?

1−7.   What is to be done to tackle this problem?

1−7−1. How must the different tasks be organized to permit them to be achieved? Can it be done?

1−7−3. What performance standards are you going to apply? How will you measure these?

1−7−4. Where is it to be done?

1−7−5. When is it to be done?

1−7−6. What are the time dimensions?

1−7−7. What functional areas, departments, etc., will be included and/or affected?

1−7−8. How will you know when you have done it? How will you tell if you are falling behind or heading for failure?

2.   SET PROJECT OR SOLUTION OBJECTIVES (P)

2−1.   What is your general objective?

2−1−1. Do you have clear exactly what it is you are trying to achieve? What general state of affairs are you trying to bring about?

2−1−2. What are your short term aims?

2−1−3. What are your long term aims?

2−1−4. Are your objectives realistic? For yourself? For others involved?

2−1−5. What general guidelines will you be following?

2−1−6. What do your goals imply? What tasks do they lead to and within what time frame?

2−1−7. Is there a different way of describing your objectives? Perhaps a different statement, angle, or viewpoint will lead to different ideas for solutions?

2−1−8. Are your objectives in any way ambiguous, conflicting, or inconsistent?

2−1−9. Do those involved have a shared and agreed view of the objectives?

2−2. What are your specific objectives?

2−2−1. What are the specific characteristics of the situation you wish to bring about?

2−2−2. What will be the criteria for success? How will you decide when the problem is satisfactorily solved or your goal reached?

2−2−3. What real world actions, goals, attitudes, or modes of behavior do the general ideals or objectives imply? What will have to happen? To what requirements for performance, behavior and design characteristics do the objectives lead?

2−2−4. What degree of success are you aiming for?

2−2−5. What degree of success will you be satisfied with?

2−2−6. Which will be the key characteristics of success? Which will be the less important characteristics?

2−2−7. What is the least you *must* do?

2−2−8. What is the most you *can* do?

2−2−9. How soon do you want it done?

2−3. How can you gain the maximum contribution from solving this problem?

2−3−1. Are you sure this is what you really want, or what is really needed?

2−3−2. How can you turn what is happening into a situation in which you or others involved can grow and expand potential?

2−3−3. How might you turn any difficulties to your advantage? What new opportunities might there be? How might these be exploited?

2−3−4. Have you detected and acknowledged your strengths and weaknesses—or those of others involved—and planned around them?

2−3−5. In the event of being able to accomplish only some of your objectives, what are your priorities?

2−3−6. Do you have alternate goals? If you cannot achieve one, would another be satisfactory?

2−3−7. How many different paths might lead to your objectives? Are some more appealing, more effective, more motivating, more fruitful, more economical, faster, less troublesome than others?

2−3−8. How might they all compare? How might you select?

3. PLAN ORGANIZATION OF OPERATION (P, SB)

3−1. As a result of the objectives. where might effort best be directed?

3−1−1. What areas are there?

3−1−2. Do they all have to be covered at this point?

3−1−3. Can they all be covered? If not, which merit the most effort at this point, or which arrangement of fragments is most appropriate?

3−1−4. Which areas need the most effort, the most time, the most watching, the most thought?

3−1−5. Which activities have important sequencing or timing constraints?

3−1−6. Which activities are the most flexible, the easiest to accommodate?

3−1−7. Which activities are most subject to uncertainty?

3−1−8. Which activities will have the greatest impact if they are delayed, fail, or succeed?

3−1−9. Who can help you with this?

3−2. How should effort be organized?

3−2−1. What sequence of actions is required? What timing is required?

3−2−2. How must the different tasks be organized to permit them to be achieved? Can it be done?

3−2−3. How long will each action take? If this is not known, how will it affect the way things fit together? What precautions will need to be taken?

3−2−4. Are there any fundamentally important activities?

3−2−5. What steps will you take to make sure that the separate parts of the project interlink smoothly?

3−2−6. What alternatives are there in the event of failure along the way to each target?

3−2−7. What can be arranged to allow reorganization and adaptation to failure?

3−2−8. What can be arranged to permit taking advantage of an unexpected opportunity or reversal?

3−2−9. Are there any activities which could suddenly become vital? Is there enough flexibility to allow these to be accommodated?

3−2−10. What techniques can you use to sort all this out and keep it straight? Make lists? Draw diagrams? Use mathematical or planning techniques?

3−3.   How can maximum output be attained?

3−3−1. What has to be done to push this through fast?

3−3−2. How can impetus be maintained? What or whom can you use to keep the pressure on?

3−3−3. How can separate parts or people support, motivate, or boost each other?

3−3−4. Can you get momentum or inertial force into this?

3−3−5. How can morale, resiliance, and enthusiasm be maintained?

3−3−6. Is massive, steady, or intermittent effort most appropriate?

3−4.   What progress checkpoints will there be?

3−4−1. What standards of performance are you going to apply? How will you measure these?

3−4−2. How will observations be recorded and/or reported?

3−4−3. What target dates, target amounts, or target positions are there?

3−4−4. What are the timing and target priorities?

3−4−5. How will you know if things start to go wrong?

3−4−6. How will you arrange affairs to prevent things going wrong?

3−4−7. What will you do in case of emergency? How will you organize yourself, what will you have ready to put into action?

3−4−8. How quickly can decisions be made?

3−4−9. How sensitive to the presence and anticipation of problems will this operation be?

3−5. What team structure will provide the best arrangement of people and services to do the job?

3−5−1. What will be the individual objectives, responsibilities, scope, privileges, and authority?

3−5−2. What relationships should exist within the team, and between the team and others involved?

3−5−3. Are all those involved fully aware of the problem-solving plan and what it means?

3−5−4. Is anyone else working on thsi very same problem, and, if so, can you pool resources or otherwise benefit?

3−6. What is the extent and what are the limitations of the project?

3−6−1. What is to be done to tackle this problem?

3−6−2. When is it to be done?

3−6−3. What are the time dimensions?

3−6−4. Where is it to be done?

3−6−5. How is it to be done?

3−6−6. What functional areas, departments, etc., will be included and/or affected?

4. SELECT APPROPRIATE TECHNIQUES (P,D,IG,SB,SA)

4−1. What style of operating, approach, or behavior, is most appropriate to each phase of the problem-solving process, or to this kind of problem?

4−1−1. Is this situation full of change and uncertainty and hard to understand or control, or is it placid and easy to pin down and amenable to well-known techniques—or somewhere in between?

4−1−2. What previous knowledge or experience can be called upon, and where can this be obtained?

4−1−3. What techniques do you know whose strong points match the areas of difficulty of this problem?

4−1−4. Is there a technique which could take care of most of this problem-solving process?

4−1−5. Could this particular problem-solving process be adjusted profitably to take advantage of such a technique?

4−1−6. Will you be best served in this situation by visual imagery, verbal or mathematical techniques, graphs, flow charts, therapeutic methods, models, simulations, creativity techniques, gaming, intuition, analysis, logic, exploratory techniques or attitudes, and so on—and in what, if any mix?

4−2.   At what points in the process and at what levels will your selected approaches or techniques be used?

4−2−1. What grouping of problem-solving tools will serve best?

4−2−2. What, if any, technique is especially appropriate to each phase of the problem?

4−2−3. Have you selected a technique which has any dubious potential or drawbacks?

4−2−4. Do you really know enough about the technique or approach you have selected, or should you obtain assistance?

4−2−5. Are your techniques unnecessarily tedious, or cumbersome, complicated, imprecise, expensive, lengthy, too precise, or simplistic; or in some other way inappropriate?

4−2−6. If you use this technique what other information will you need? What other steps will you need to take?

4−2−7. Do you have the right kind of data to use this problem-solving technique?

5.   SET UP PROJECT TEAM (P,SB)

5−1.   Who will be on the team?

5−1−1. What skills are required? Who has these? Can these people be brought into the problem?

5—1—2. What previous knowledge or experience can be called upon, and where can this be obtained?

5—1—3. Is anyone else working on this very same problem and, if so, can you pool resources or otherwise benefit?

5—1—4. Do you have, or can you obtain, expert knowledge in the areas concerned?

5—1—5. Do you have, or can you obtain, someone with an imaginative, productive mind?

5—1—6. Do you have, or can you obtain, someone of mature judgment and analytical bent?

5—1—7. Do you have, or can you obtain, a skilful organizer and adept tactician?

5—1—8. Do you have, or can you obtain, a good synthesizer?

5—1—9. Can you match the people with the task requirements and will they cooperate well?

5—2.   What team structure will provide the best arrangement of people and services to do the job?

5—2—1. What relationships should exist within the team, and between the team and others involved?

5—2—2. What will be the individual objectives, responsibilities, scope, privileges, and authority?

5—2—3. Will those involved have access to appropriate information in order to make decisions?

5—2—4. Is the effort really structured properly? Will those involved have too many decisions to make in a short time, thus increasing stress? Will they have too many fluctuations in work flow? Or too few?

5—2—5. Will you be able to arrange conditions conducive to successful problem solving?

5—2—6. How will the team be motivated to make their best effort?

6.   PROJECT INTO THE FUTURE (P,D)

6—1.   What might happen next?—in the short term?—in the long term?

6—1—1. Is there some reason why the future in this situation may differ considerably from the past?

6–1–2. Can you figure out what will replace the present situation and its solution?

6–1–3. When might events in other areas alter the shape of this problem?

6–1–4. How are future developments likely to affect this system?

6–2.   How are you looking ahead? What techniques are you using?

6–2–1. Are you constructing scenarios?

6–2–2. Are you projecting present trends, either statistically or intuitively?

6–2–3. Are you eliciting expert opinion?

6–2–4. Are you looking far enough ahead?

6–2–5. What are your long term aims?

6–2–6. What would happen if the problem situation doubled itself, stopped, reversed, or increased tenfold?

6–2–7. What will happen in other areas when you initiate activity in the areas you are working on? What are the implications and ramifiations?

6–3.   Will this situation still be operating like this in the future?

6–3–1. What are the growing edges of the situation for which the solution is to be designed? How many are there? How do they interact? How interdependent are their growth rates? How vigorous is their growth? Which ones will present the most serious problems for your solution? How might your solution have to cope with them?

6–3–2. If there is uncertainty in the situation, is it completely uncertain and completely unpredictable, is it uncertain within certain limits, or can some kind of probability be assigned to the situation?

6–3–3. In what way do the values of variables or elements, quantities, qualities, or characteristics, change with time? What specific values or ranges of values do they assume?

6–3–4. Can you imagine several different futures? What if something entirely different happens?

6–3–5. In looking ahead, what kinds of problems might you come across for which your approach or your way of operating would be inadequate or useless?

6−3−6. Why is the framework containing this problem structured the way it is? Can this be changed? Will it change anyway? What will happen if it does?

6−3−7. Have you considered ramifications outside the immediate problem area?

7. SET STANDARDS AND SUCCESS CRITERIA (P,SB)

7−1. What will be your criteria for success? How will you decide when the problem is satisfactorily solved or your goal reached?

7−1−1. What will be the key characteristics of success? What will be the less important characteristics?

7−1−2. What would be the ideal? How close can you get? Can you think of how you could conceivably overcome those last obstacles to attaining the ideal?

7−1−3. What is the least you *must* do?

7−1−4. What is the most you *can* do?

7−1−5. What level of performance are you aiming for?

7−1−6. How well do you expect your project to do in terms of speed, depth of investigation, scope of conclusions? What other qualities, criteria, values, aims are involved?

7−1−7. Have you established rules, tests, or guidelines for deciding between alternatives?

7−2. What do your goals imply? What tasks do they lead to, and within what time frame?

7−2−1. Which real world actions, goals, attitudes, or modes of behavior do the general ideals or objectives imply? What will have to happen? To what requirements for performance, behavior, and design characteristics do the objectives lead?

7−2−2. What special characteristics does this operation or situation have? What needs to be done to accommodate or take advantage of these?

7−2−3. How well must your solution perform with respect to adaptability to difficulties, speed of coping with problems, speed of decision making, and speed and flexibility of information flow?

7−2−4. How well must your solution perform in terms of, for example, speed, humanity, cost, environmental or political impact, range of impact? Or what other qualities, criteria, values, aims, will be reflected?

7-2-5. How will you decide what tests to use to assess your solution?

7-2-6. What tests will you set up, what feedback will you devise, what measures will you take to ensure that your criteria are met?

7-2-7. What will you be weighing and assessing to determine a solution's acceptability?

7-3.   What progress checkpoints will there be?

7-3-1. What standards of performance are you going to apply? How will you measure these?

7-3-2. How will observations be recorded and/or reported?

7-3-3. What target dates, target amounts, or target positions are there?

7-3-4. What are the timing and target priorities?

7-3-5. How will you know if things start to go wrong?

7-3-6. How will you arrange affairs to prevent things going wrong?

8.   QUESTION ASSUMPTIONS (P,D,IG,SB,SA,AA)

8-1.   Can you be certain that the problem is what it seems to be? Are you sure *this* is the real problem?

8-1-1. Is there anything here that is so much a part of the accepted way of looking at things that you are very unlikely to even notice it as questionable?

8-1-2. Why do you think this problem is worth solving? Are your reasons really valid?

8-1-3. What unwarranted assumptions are you making? Can you list *all* the assumptions you are making—especially those too obvious to question—and examine each one?

8-1-4. What assumptions are you making about the larger situation or system, the background against which this difficulty is happening? Are they valid?

8-1-5. Are you carrying over an inappropriate set of expectations into this situation—concerning results, your own behavior, behavior of others, the future, capacities, capabilities?

8−1−6. What unquestioned assumptions have you made about, for example, the environment, political aspects, personal factors, technological aspects, the future, present trends, economic aspects, skills, training, policy, organization, and so on?

8−1−7. What value systems, beliefs, or attitudes are you assuming to be implicit in this situation? Are these assumptions valid?—Could this change? What would be the effects?

8−1−8. Are there any parts you see as difficulties which you *could* see as non-problems, or vice versa?

8−1−9. What are you refusing to acknowledge?

8−2.   Are you approaching this in a way which will allow you to find the truth, or to find what you would like to find?

8−2−1. Are all your facts and interpretations correct?

8−2−2. How do you know your facts are correct?

8−2−3. Is any of your information in any way suspect? If so, reestablish the "facts" involved. Does your new information lead to any different interpretations?

8−2−4. Look at your "reliable sources." Are they?

8−2−5. Could someone be deliberately or accidentally misleading you?

8−2−6. Are you sure you have all the information you need?

8−2−7. Is there anything you consistently overlook, don't pay much attention to, emphasize, or concentrate on when looking at problems? How is that affecting this situation?

8−2−8. Maybe you have all this back to front?

8−3.   How can you make it all look different?

8−3−1. Can you change one of your assumptions about the structure of this situation?

8−3−2. Is there a way to leave the facts the same but see them differently?

8−3−3. Can you change one of your assumptions as to how this situation fits into the larger picture?

8−3−4. Can you start from somewhere else?

8−3−5. Are you dealing with this problem at the right levels? Have you looked at this problem at different levels? Have you looked at it from enough viewpoints—for example, from the viewpoints of personality, organization, esthetics, timing, motivation, information, energy, production, finance?

8-3-6. Would any of the above viewpoints change your perception of the problem—making it more simple, complex, understandable, or challenging?

8-3-7. Can you change the level at which you are looking at this? For example, if you have to invent a new agricultural tractor, would it help to think instead of new types of cultivation, or, alternatively, of new types of motive power or drive systems? Can you take a wider view, or more specific views?

9.   DEVISE APPROPRIATE TESTS (P,D,SA)

9-1.   What tests will you set up?—what feedback will you devise?—what measures will you take?

9-1-1. What special characteristics does this situation or operation have? What needs to be done to accommodate or take advantage of these?

9-1-2. How much testing is possible, appropriate, realistic, wise?

9-1-3. How will you decide if the cost of your enquiry exceeds the value of solving the problem?

9-1-4. How will you decide when you have a fair grasp of the problem? Are you taking care not to miss anything, but not being so inclusive that you are overloaded with possibilities?

9-1-5. How will you deal with conflicting objectives and values?

9-1-6. In testing, are you looking for disconfirming instances or are you looking for corroboration? Doing the latter can be misleading and miss loopholes.

9-2.   How are you going to test the validity of your hypotheses, ideas, concepts, or solutions?

9-2-1. How will you test what might happen to these in the future?

9-2-2. How are you going to test the impact of psychological, ecological, political, economic, or technological aspects, now and in the projected future?

9-2-3. How accurately can you determine the symptoms?

9−2−4. At what stage or stages should the tests be applied?

9−2−5. How will the tests actually be implemented?

9−2−6. How will you know if your tests are adequate? How will you test the tests?

9−2−7. How much can you find out or do without disturbing the situation?

9−2−8. How subject to misinterpretation might your tests of your solution be?

9−3. What will you be weighing and assessing to determine a solution's acceptability?

9−3−1. Has a program been developed to assess the solution's success?

9−3−2. How will you decide what tests to use to assess your solution?

9−3−3. How far can you test your solution before actually putting it into effect?

9−3−4. How will you decide if the solution passes satisfactorily the tests set for it?

9−3−5. How are you going to test the logical, practical structure of your solution or model?

9−3−6. Can you imagine a disaster for your solution? How would you avoid such a disaster?

9−3−7. How many ways can you think of to put your solution out of joint? How can you alter circumstances to test it?

10.   ASSESS APPROACH SO FAR (P,D,IG,SB,SA,AA)

10−1. Are you making a genuine advance?

10−1−1. Are the activities underway adequate?

10−1−2. Are the activities underway related as closely as possible to the objectives?

10−1−3. Is enough being done?

10−1−4. Is what is being done being done well enough?

10−1−5. Are you getting enough feedback, response, contribution?

10−1−6. Are you communicating effectively, appealingly, honestly?

10-1-7. Are the overall objectives being attained?

10-1-8. Is the situation changing such that:

    a. Tactics need to be changed?

    b. Overall strategy needs to be changed?

    c. Overall objectives need to be changed?

10-1-9. Can you minimize activities that do not contribute directly to overall objectives? Can you maximize those that do?

10-2. **Is this the most effective way to do this? Is this the best action you could be taking?**

10-2-1. Could you do this faster? Could you have this done sooner?

10-2-2. Are you wasting time anywhere?

10-2-3. Do you need to speed up or slow down?

10-2-4. Are you covering this in sufficient depth?

10-2-5. Are you making a genuine contribution?

10-2-6. Are you dissipating your efforts? Could your work be more concentrated?

10-2-7. Is anything in jeopardy?

10-3. **Are things keeping moving and coordinated?**

10-3-1. Is anything getting out of control? Organization, speed, concentration, resiliance, timing, imagination, criticism?

10-3-2. Is any activity blocked, losing momentum, or likely to?

10-3-3. If so, what can be done to evade the blockage or regain momentum?

10-3-4. What would be the effect on other activities of clearing the block, or increasing momentum—or failing to?

10-3-5. What arrangement of activities or effort can be made to permit maximum progress? Is there anything that can be left, suspended, or slowed down to permit redirection of effort?

10-3-6. Can effort be reduced in any area?

10-3-7. Could a rearrangement of effort permit all activities to continue optimally?

10-3-8. Would any of these rearrangements violate any of the objectives?

10−4. Do you need help or redirection?

10−4−1. Do you need a morale boost? Do you need improved resiliance? Can friends help?

10−4−2. Are you trying to do too much, or are you making rash responses to stress or to sudden uncontrolled change?

10−4−3. Are you staying organized? Do you need some new metaphor, some new pattern, some new ideal, some new picture of your role or of the situation to help you stay on top of things?

10−4−4. Are you carrying an inappropriate set of expectations into this situation—concerning results, your own behavior, behavior of others, the future, capacities, capabilities?

10−4−5. Have you selected a technique with any dubious potential or drawbacks?

10−4−6. Are your techniques unnecessarily tedious or imprecise? Or are they too precise? Or inappropriate?

10−4−7. Do you really know enough about the technique or approach you have selected, or should you obtain assistance?

10−4−8. Is this problem solving or: panic, self-justification, avoidance, rationalization; or . . .?

10−5. What have you missed?

10−5−1. Is this doomed from the start?

10−5−2. What is there that you don't know or are unsure of?

10−5−3. Are you hoping that this will turn out, even though it would require good luck rather than good management?

10−5−4. Are you closing your eyes to anything?

10−5−5. Could someone be deliberately or accidentally misleading you?

10−5−6. Are you part of the problem?

10−5−7. Are you afraid to throw it all out and start again?

10−5−8. What puzzles you?

10−6. Is this going to affect something else?

10−6−1. To what degree is this linked to, approaching, or on a collision course with anything else?

10−6−2. How can it be affected by anything else linked to it?

10−6−3. How can it affect anything else linked to it?

10−6−4. When and why might this occur?

10−6−5. How and with what results?

10−6−6. What would be done in such an eventuality?

10−7. How could you achieve more penetrating insights?

10−7−1. Have you included some means of, or technique for, seeing your problem from different viewpoints?

10−7−2. Have you made sure that imaginative, intuitive, and speculative elements are present to balance the analytic, rational, judgmental elements in your approach?

10−7−3. Have you assessed the probability of difficulties for your solution or approach, and planned or modified it accordingly?

10−7−4. Are there any steps in your problem solving that could be eliminated, reversed, changed, or added to?

10−7−5. Don't you really need a broader outlook? Are you looking at the situation from too limited a perspective?

10−7−6. Should you draw in your horns and look at a smaller range of events?

10−7−7. Could you operate with benefit at a higher level?

10−7−8. Could you achieve more wide ranging syntheses?

10−7−9. Should a larger, encompassing problem be attacked?

10−8. What are the strengths and weaknesses of this approach? What are you overlooking?

10−8−1. Are you working in areas of maximum contribution potential?

10−8−2. Do you have your priorities right?

10−8−3. Are you avoiding triviality and superficiality in all places?

10−8−4. What could be a source of difficulty with this approach? Personal—attempting too much, procrastinating, avoiding difficulties, unethical? Conceptual—unrealistic, impractical, overcomplicated, simplistic? Organizational—inappropriate to the day-to-day, business, or political realities?

10−8−5. Is there a more bold or adventurous way of doing this?

10−8−6. Can you think of any possible disadvantages of having taken this approach with this problem?

10−8−7. Are you indulging in "overkill?" Is your approach unnecessarily cumbersome or complicated?

10−8−8. Are you using the most up-to-date, sophisticated, advanced model or approach to your problem? If not, could you use it? How could you find out? How could you learn to use it?

10−8−9. Is there a unifying theme, central concept, idea, or analogy which permits this strategy to be easily borne in mind and employed? Or might you lose track of what you are trying to do?

10−9.   Can you go any further with your strategy at this point? Should you wait until you find out more about the situation?

10−9−1. Have you planned as far as it is possible to plan, given the circumstances?

10−9−2. If your strategy is incomplete, do you have a reserve plan to fall back upon in case of emergency?

10−9−3. Is this an old strategy? Perhaps an old strategy would work well in this situation, but can you devise a strategy which would be even better?

10−9−4. Are all those involved fully aware of the problem-solving plan and what it means?

10−9−5. Could you perceive the situation in an entirely different way and build a superior strategy?

10−9−6. Can you think of an entirely new kind of approach?

10−9−7. Are you doing too much too soon?

10−9−8. Are you doing too little too late?

10−10.   Is your strategy still appropriate to the problem situation?

10−10−1. Are you changing tactics too often? Are you losing your grip on the situation?

10−10−2. Are you managing to keep a clear picture of the parts of the situation? Can you detect uneven progress or the approach of trouble?

10–10–3. Do you need to do the same things but organize them better?

10–10–4. Are you keeping in mind the objectives for solving this problem, or is technique or a particular aspect of the problem clouding your vision?

10–10–5. Have there been any surprises? If so, why?

10–10–6. Look at the points where you didn't feel so sure of yourself. Why was this? Is it important? What can you do about it?

10–10–7. Have you been acting in a flexible, imaginative, adaptive, inventive, coherent manner? Would anyone else agree with your answer? Ask them.

10–10–8. Are you taking the same approach as usual in solving this one?

10–10–9. Has your conception of the situation changed to the extent that your approach must change?

11.   BASIC FACT FINDING (D, SA)

11–1.   What is involved?

11–1–1. What is the overall situation?

11–1–2. What are the major trends?—What are some of the minor trends?—What forecasts have been made?

11–1–3. What are the components of this problem? How many are there?

11–1–4. What are the attributes or characteristics of these components?

11–1–5. What are the most significant, important, or urgent aspects of this problem? Why?

11–1–6. How complex does this problem seem to be? How many parts and levels does it seem to have?

11–1–7. Are time and change important in this situation? Is the situation dynamic?

11–1–8. Does this involve any deeper issues?

11–1–9. Is it really more complicated than this? Or more simple?

11–2.   As a result of the objectives, where might effort best be directed?

11–2–1. What areas are there?

11−2−2. Do they all have to be covered at this point?

11−2−3. Can they all be covered? If not, which merit the most effort at this point, or which arrangements of fragments are most appropriate?

11−2−4. Which areas need the most effort, the most time, the most watching, or the most thought?

11−2−5. Which activities have important sequencing or timing constraints?

11−2−6. Which activities are the most flexible, the easiest to accommodate?

11−2−7. Which activities are the most subject to uncertainty?

11−2−8. Which activities will have the greatest impact if they are delayed, fail, or succeed?

11−2−9. Who can help you with this?

11−3.   What kind of problem does this seem to be? For example, is it emotional, political, organizational, theoretical, technical, financial, psychological, medical, or other?—or what blend of various factors?

11−3−1. What puzzles you?

11−3−2. What principles are involved?

11−3−3. Where does this problem fit in the general scheme of things?

11−3−4. Is this part of a larger system or problem, and closely connected to it?

11−3−5. What other systems, structures, or frameworks directly influence or are influenced by this system?

11−3−6. How many different kinds of solution to this problem might there be?

11−3−7. How many different principles and processes seem to be involved?

11−3−8. What type of solution are you looking for here, e.g.:

    a. An operational plan of some duration?
    b. An invention or new idea?
    c. A decision-making system or organizational structure?
    d. A conceptual structure or theory?
    e. A project plan?
    f. A search for specific information?
    g. Or what?

11−4.   What is being done? What action is being taken?

11−4−1. Why is it being done?

11−4−2. How is it being done?

11−4−3. When is it being done?

11−4−4. Where is it being done?

11−4−5. To whom is it being done?

11−4−6. Can you get involved in the situation and experience the problem first-hand? Might this lead to disagreement with previous assessments of the situation both by yourself and by others?

11−5.   What is happening? What difficulties are there?—what opportunities?

11−5−1. Why is it all happening?

11−5−2. Where is it happening?

11−5−3. When is it happening?

11−5−4. How is it happening?

11−5−5. What is the timing and duration of events?

11−5−6. How fast are things happening?

11−5−7. Who is doing it?

11−5−8. Who is causing it?

11−5−9. If there is uncertainty in the situation, is it completely uncertain and completely unpredictable, is it uncertain within particular limits, or can some kind of probability be assigned to the situation?

11−6.   What are the major variables and decision sequences?

11−6−1. What routines are being followed?

11−6−2. What attitudes are involved?

11−6−3. What functions seem to be involved?

11−6−4. What values are involved?

11−6−5. What legal, financial, psychological, or other requirements are there?

11−6−6. Is there anything, any relationship, value, structural framework, process, or pattern which remains the same over any significant period of time?

11−6−7. Which elements or aspects are involved in any pattern you see?

11−6−8. Are all elements equally involved?

11−6−9. What and where are the weak points?

11−6−10. What and where are the strong points?

11−6−11. What have you missed?

12.   AVAILABLE KNOWLEDGE REVIEW (D,SA)

12−1.   What previous knowledge or experience can be called upon?—where can this be obtained?

12−1−1. What do you already know? What information is immediately available?

12−1−2. What experiences have other people had who have gone through this kind of thing? What did they learn? How can you find out?

12−1−3. What has been said about it, done about it, or written about it?

12−1−4. What similar problems have you come across?

12−1−5. Is there a parallel that can be drawn from the past?

12−1−6. Who else has had this problem or a problem anything like it?

12−1−7. Is anyone else working on this very same problem and, if so, can you pool resources or otherwise benefit?

12−1−8. Who could give you another viewpoint on this situation?

12−1−9. Where is the best place nearest you for learning about a problem like this? Can you go there? Can you contact people there? Could they help?

12−1−10. Where is the best place in the world for learning about a problem like this? Can you go there? Can you contact people there? Could they help?

12−2.   How do you know you have good information?

12−2−1. Is any of your information in any way suspect? If so, reestablish the "facts" involved. Does your new information lead to any different interpretations?

12–2–2. What information have you that negates any of these interpretations?

12–2–3. Have your "facts" been corroborated by additional sources or means?

12–2–4. What have you missed?

12–2–5. How do you know you've tried hard enough to get a current and accurate picture?

12–2–6. Are you sure you have all the information you need?

12–2–7. Have you checked it even though it might seem obvious?

12–2–8. What contradictions or inconsistencies can you see?

12–2–9. What are the latest developments, theories, and experiences in the area in which this problem is happening, or in contiguous areas?

13. LOOK AT THE HISTORY OF THE SITUATION (D,SA)

13–1.   Has it always been like this?

13–1–1. How were the present relationships or arrangements of events brought about? How did things get to be this way?

13–1–2. At what rate did this develop?

13–1–3. How long has it been going on?

13–1–4. Did the problem happen gradually or suddenly?

13–1–5. Has this problem been occurring continuously or intermittently?

13–1–6. Has the problem occurred regularly or irregularly?

13–1–7. In what way have the values of variables or elements, quantities, qualities, or characteristics, changed with time? What specific values or ranges of values have they assumed?

13–2.   What is the history of the system which contains this problem?

13–2–1. What growth, change, decay, and evolutionary patterns are evident?

13–2–2. What seem to be the significant events, trends, personages, and influences involved?

13−2−3. Has this been the only problem of its kind, or have there been others?

13−2−4. Is this situation enmeshed in difficulties of a different kind?

13−2−5. What has been the real source of trouble? What has been the principal guiding factor?

13−2−6. Will attempts to deal with this difficulty turn out to be a waste of time when the historical path of this situation is considered?

13−2−7. Has this problem had serious repercussions in other areas? With what effects? What action has been taken in response?

13−2−8. Does consideration of the past highlight any potential problems or developments?

14. DETERMINE OBJECTIVES IMPLICIT, HIDDEN, OR IMBEDDED IN THE SITUATION (D)

14−1. What are the objectives of this operation, framework, structure, or system?

14−1−1. Do we have to look outside this situation to find the objectives or the motivating or controlling forces?

14−1−2. What really motivates activity in this situation?

14−1−3. What short-term aims are implied, stated, or evident in the situation? What is regarded as successful?

14−1−4. What long-term aims are implied, stated, or evident in the situation? What provides fulfilment?

14−1−5. What priorities are implied, stated, or evident in the situation?

14−1−6. Why is all this happening? Why is it being done?

14−1−7. What principles are involved?

14−1−8. What degree of success is aimed for?

14−1−9. Are the objectives appropriate to the situation?

14−1−10. Which real world actions, goals, attitudes, or modes of behavior do the general ideals or objectives imply? What will have to happen? To what requirements for performance, behavior, and design characteristics do the objectives lead?

14−1−11. What do your goals imply? What tasks do they lead to and within what time frame?

14-2.   What hidden or unstated objectives might there be?

14-2-1.   Is the justification for this system to be found in some other area?

14-2-2.   Are the real objectives disguised by the expressed objectives?

14-2-3.   Why might the real objectives be hidden? Is this a good thing or a bad thing?

14-2-4.   Are any objectives hidden for the purpose of deliberately misleading people?

14-2-5.   Are any objectives hidden accidentally or unconsciously, and in need of exposure and discussion?

14-2-6.   Are the objectives of different parts of the problem area, or of the system which contains the problem, consistent? Do any areas conflict with each other?

14-2-7.   Do stated objectives conflict with what is actually happening? If so, deliberately or accidentally?

14-2-8.   If stated objectives differ from actual motivations, is this because the situation has evolved with time, and formal expressions of objectives have not kept pace?

15.   DETERMINE INFORMATION AND DECISION-MAKING STRUCTURES (D)

15-1.   What communication is going on?

15-1-1.   What information is being transmitted and received?

15-1-2.   Who is transmitting and receiving information?

15-1-3.   When is information being received or transmitted?

15-1-4.   From where is information being transmitted and to where?

15-1-5.   At which points is information being received and from where?

15-1-6.   How much information is being transmitted or received and in what patterns?

15-1-7.   What is the structure of the information?—How is it arranged, organized, sequenced?

15-1-8.   How quickly can information be obtained?

15-1-9.   How fast does information travel?

15-1-10.   How frequently is information needed?

15−2.   How is information handled or processed?

15−2−1. Why is information being transmitted and received?

15−2−2. How is information being transmitted and received? What is its impact?

15−2−3. What happens when the information reaches its destination? How much is used for decision making?—How much for reference only?—How much is kept?—How much is not used?

15−2−4. If there is redundancy or excessive traffic, is this useful or unnecessary, or does it cover some other problem?

15−2−5. What is the content of each message in terms of information, form, and function?

15−2−6. What are the components of this message?

15−2−7. How does this message fit into the decision-making or operating structure?

15−2−8. To whom is the message addressed?

15−2−9. Is the message primarily for decision making, for learning, or for speculatory purposes, or is it multi-purpose?

15−2−10. Is the method of communication appropriate? Does the message reach the receiver in suitable form?

15−3.   What decision-making structure is involved?

15−3−1. How does the decision-making structure work? How are decisions made? With what impact?

15−3−2. How cumbersome, effective, responsive, disorganized, or to the point is the decision-making process in general?

15−3−3. What decision-making tools and techniques are used? Are they appropriate? Up to date? Properly used?

15−3−4. Who is involved in the decision-making structure?

15−3−5. What information supports what decision making, and how effectively?

15−3−6. Does information go where it is needed? Does any go where it is not needed?

15−3−7. How many decisions are made without full information? If information is not available, is this because the situation is fast-moving, uncertain, or risky? Is it because of inefficiency or poor planning?

Or is it just not feasible to obtain the information? What can be done?

15−3−8. How quickly can decisions be made?

15−3−9. Why are the decisions being made?

15−3−10. Why are decisions being made this way?

16. EXAMINE PARTS AND INTERRELATIONSHIPS (D,SB)

16−1. **What relationship does each part have with each other part?**

16−1−1. What is connected to what? Can you draw a map or pitcure of the pieces? How is each one connected, or how should or could it be, to the others? Are there any missing connections?

16−1−2. What are the most important parts, relationships, outcomes?

16−1−3. What specific influences are at work? Which might operate in your favor, or in favor of the system's objectives? Which may operate against you or the system?

16−1−4. What might be some of the long-term ramifications, influences, and interrelationships?

16−1−5. What can be inferred from this? What is implied by this?

16−1−6. What groups, categories, or types of elements and what groups, categories, or types of relationships can be classed together? What characteristics are shared?

16−1−7. How many groups, categories, or types of elements and relationships are there?

16−1−8. How many groupings, classifications, or types are mutually exclusive?

16−1−9. How many groupings, classifications, or types overlap?

16−1−10. Is this the best way of grouping these elements and relationships? How else could it be done?

16−2. **Which occurrences are associated with which other occurrences?**

16−2−1. What else is connected to this, either directly or indirectly?

16−2−2. What is the nature or manner of these connections?

16−2−3. How closely connected to this situation are these other events, principles, functions, concepts?

16−2−4. How strongly do associated occurrences interact?

16−2−5. What events include, or form a necessary part of, other events?

16−2−6. When do parts get out of step?

16−2−7. Why are things related to each other in the ways they are?

16−2−8. How were the present relationships or arrangements of events brought about?

16−2−9. Who is involved in more than one part?

16−3.   Is this going to affect something else?

16−3−1. To what degree is this linked to, approaching, or on a collision course with anything else?

16−3−2. How can it be affected by anything else linked to it?

16−3−3. How can it affect anything else linked to it?

16−3−4. When and why might this occur?

16−3−5. How and with what results?

16−3−6. What would be done in such an eventuality?

16−4.   Do all these elements or parts form a coherent structure—that is, do all their relationships, or apparent relationships, make sense?—does the whole thing make sense?

16−4−1. Is there anything, any relationship, value, or structural framework which remains the same over any significant period of time?

16−4−2. Are the relationships always the same, or do they change, oscillate, fluctuate?

16−4−3. Are any connections permanent and stable?—Are any intermittent, chancy, arbitrary or irregular?

16−4−4. In what way do the values of variables or elements, qualities, and characteristics change with time? What specific value or values do they assume?

16−4−5. Are connections one-way only, two-way, or variable?

16−4−6. Is there a hierarchy of connections, or do all events exert similar influence?

16—5. What is the best way to express the relationships involved—that is, mathematically, psychologically, qualitatively, or what?

16—5—1. To what extent is it possible to make a formal mathematical, quantitative, logical) statement of the relationships between variables or parts of the problem?

16—5—2. Is there a principal focus of complexity?

16—5—3. If one group of elements or relationships were removed, how would this affect the other groups?

16—5—4. What duration, cost, urgency, potential, and priority are associated with each component or relationship?

16—5—5. What makes you think that you have the right view of the relationships involved?

17. LOOK AT NEIGHBORING SYSTEMS (D,SB)

17—1. Where does this problem fit in the general scheme of things?

17—1—1. What other systems, structures, or frameworks directly influence, or are influenced by, this system?

17—1—2. What other systems, structures, or frameworks are indirectly connected to this system?

17—1—3. How does this problem relate to and compare with other problems and events?

17—1—4. Which systems or events control, influence, or motivate others?

17—1—5. Are these influences continuous, periodic, sporadic, random, intermittent?

17—1—6. Are these influences able to be controlled or altered?

17—1—7. How are the related systems developing?

17—1—8. Is anything getting out of step?

17—2. What traffic or interchange is there between this situation and its surroundings?

17—2—1. Which are the more important parts, relationships, outcomes?

17—2—2. What specific influences are at work? Which might operate in your favor or in favor of the system's objectives? Which may operate against you or the system?

17–2–3. What might be some of the long-term ramifications, influences, and interrelationships?

17–2–4. What can be inferred from this? What is implied by this?

17–2–5. Are the relationships always the same, or do they change, oscillate, fluctuate?

17–2–6. Are any connections permanent and stable?—Are any intermittent, chancy, arbitrary or irregular?

17–2–7. In what way do the values of variables or elements, quantities, qualities, and characteristics change with time? What specific values or ranges do they assume?

17–2–8. Are the connections one-way only, two-way, or variable?

17–2–9. Is there a hierarchy of connections, or do all events exert similar influence?

17–3.   Why does the framework which contains this problem interact the way it does with other systems? Can this be changed?

17–3–1. Why is the framework which contains this problem structured the way it is? Can this be changed? Will it change anyway? What will happen if it does?

17–3–2. What new arrangement of larger systems could make this problem disappear?

17–3–3. Against what political, organizational, policy, or ideological background will your solution be built? How will your solution fit into it?

17–3–4. Against what technological background will your solution be built? How will your solution fit into it?

17–3–5. Against what economical or financial background will your solution be built? How will your solution fit into it?

17–3–6. Against what educational or ecological background will your solution be built? How will your solution fit into it?

17–3–7. Have you considered ramifications outside the immediate problem area?

17–3–8. If the problem is organizational, have you considered emotional factors too? If it is a people problem, have you remembered costs?

18. ASSESS SYSTEM NEEDS, RESOURCE CONSUMPTION (D,SB)

18—1. How much support does this system require in terms of people's time, materials, equipment, energy, coordination, etc.?

18—1—1. How many people seem to be involved?

18—1—2. What elements or aspects are involved in any pattern you see?

18—1—3. How frequently, for what lengths of time, and how intensively does the system demand people's time, materials, equipment, energy, coordination, etc.?

18—1—4. Who is providing the greatest amount of positive, supportive, integrative energy in this system, and why? Whose efforts hold it all together and keep it moving?

18—1—5. Who is providing the least amount of positive, supportive, integrative energy in this system, and why? Who fails to contribute to keeping it all moving and growing?

18—1—6. Which part of the problem area contributes the most positive energy, and why? What holds it all together and keeps it moving and growing?

18—1—7. Is everything in balance, in harmony?

18—2. Does this system consume resources which would be better used elsewhere?

18—2—1. Does this system consume more resources than are merited by its output and value?

18—2—2. How has demand for this system for resources grown or changed? Why?

18—2—3. How will the demand by this system for resources grow or change in the future? Why?

18—2—4. What degree of irregularity of supply, interest, energy, pressure, or acceptance will cause this system to fail?

18—2—5. At what point will this system fail through too low a level of supply, energy, interest, pressure, or acceptance?

18—2—6. At what point will this system fail through too high a level of supply, energy, interest, pressure, or acceptance?

18—2—7. What would happen if the problem situation doubled itself, stopped, reversed, or increased tenfold?

19.   ASSESS DEMANDS UPON THE SYSTEM (D,SB)

19−1.   What kind of demands does this system satisfy? How important are they?

19−1−1.   Who needs this system? Who relies upon it? What services does it provide?

19−1−2.   What would happen if this system were not available? What substitutes might there be?

19−1−3.   How often is this system needed?

19−1−4.   For what duration of time and how intensively is this system needed?

19−1−5.   How has demand for this system grown or changed? Why?

19−1−6.   How will demand for this system grow or change in the future? Why?

19−2.   What would happen if the problem situation doubled itself, stopped, reversed, or increased tenfold?

19−2−1.   What is this situation or solution unprepared for?

19−2−2.   Which part of this situation is most disruptive, and why?

19−2−3.   At what point will this system fail through too high a level of demand, load, competition, pressure, stress, or change?

19−2−4.   At what point will this system fail through too low a level of demand, load, competition, pressure, stress, or change?

19−2−5.   Is the effort really structured properly? Do those involved have too many decisions to make in a short time, thus increasing stress? Do they have too many fluctuations in work flow? Or too few?

19−2−6.   What degree of irregularity of demand or load will cause this system to fail?

20.   EXAMINE OVERALL STRUCTURE OR SYSTEM (D,SB)

20−1.   What is the overall situation?

20−1−1.   What are the major trends?—What are some of the minor trends?—What forecasts have been made?

20−1−2.   Can a main focus of difficulty be isolated?

20−1−3. Can the problem be resolved into some fairly distinct categories, groups, or areas of difficulty?

20−1−4. Can the problem be broken down into smaller parts which can fairly safely be dealt with separately?

20−1−5. If so, what needs to be borne in mind, what conditions need to be met, or what objectives have to be satisfied for the sub-problems to be dealt with separately and later pulled together for the total solution?

20−1−6. Can you see any decisive patterns at all?

20−1−7. Is there anything, any relationship, value, structural framework, or pattern, which remains the same over any significant period of time?

20−1−8. Is there a principal focus of organization or control, a principal trouble spot or weak point?

20−1−9. Is this the kind of situation in which subtracting or changing just one element, or adding just one more, will radically change the character of the situation?

20−1−10. What characteristics are peculiar to the total situation? What does the whole have that the parts do not? What can it do that the pieces themselves cannot do?

20−2. Where does this problem fit in the general scheme of things?

20−2−1. Is this part of a larger system or problem, and closely connected to it?

20−2−2. What assumptions are you making about the larger system, the background against which this situation is happening? Are they valid?

20−2−3. Should a larger, encompassing problem be attacked?

20−2−4. Why is the framework containing this problem structured the way it is? Can this be changed? Will it change anyway? What will happen if it does?

20−2−5. What coordinates these events?—What are the structural characteristics?—What processes hold it all together?

20−2−6. Do all these elements or parts form a coherent structure—that is, do all their interrelationships, or apparent interrelationships, make sense? And does the whole thing make sense?

20−2−7. What are the objectives of this framework, structure, or system?

20−3. How sensitive to the presence and anticipation of problems is this system?

20−3−1. Who is responsible for, or affects, the framework, structure, or system involved?

20−3−2. What amount of planning, forecasting, and problem seeking goes on within this system? Is this a problem?

20−3−3. Who is involved in the planning, forecasting, and problem-seeking effort? Is it done well?

20−3−4. Who is causing any detrimental planning, forecasting, or problem seeking in systems affecting your situation?

20−3−5. Where is the positive, supportive, integrative energy in this system located? At what points in the process does this occur, around which elements or relationships, and at what times?

20−3−6. Are there any peaks in the disruptive activity in the system? When, how, and where do they occur?

20−3−7. Are there any peaks in the integrative activity in the system? When, how, and why do they occur?

20−3−8. Is there an "energy imbalance" in the larger system of which this process, in conjunction with its related processes, forms a part? That is, do some of the processes need to go to a lot of effort to deal with the effects of one or another of these processes?

20−3−9. If there is any "energy imbalance," is it reasonable? Couldn't it be changed? If so, in how many different ways? If not, why not? And is the reason given a real or sufficient reason?

21. FACT QUESTIONING AND ASSESSMENT (D,IG,SA)

21−1. Why do you perceive this to be a problem? What objectives are being frustrated?

21−1−1. Are there any parts you see as difficulties that you *could* see as non-problems, or vice versa?

21−1−2. Is there anything that you know, any facts or information, which could show that what is seen to be the problem really is not?

21−1−3. If you have established that a certain factor was the cause of your problem, have you established that other factors involved were *not* also causes?

21−1−4. Are you looking at information not just for what it shows to be the case, but also for what it shows to be *not* the case?

QUESTIONS FOR STRATEGY ELEMENTS

21−1−5. Is there anything here which is so much a part of the accepted way of looking at things that you are very unlikely to even notice it as possibly questionable?

21−1−6. What unwarranted assumptions are you making? Can you list *all* the assumptions you are making—especially those too obvious to question—and examine each one?

21−1−7. Can you be certain that the problem is what it seems to be? Are you sure that *this* is the real problem?

21−1−8. Have you considered ramifications outside the immediate problem area?

21−1−9. Why is this not just one problem?

21−1−10. Do you feel you have really grasped what is happening?

21−1−11. Where does this problem fit in the general scheme of things?

21−2. Are you sure you have all the information you need?

21−2−1. Is any of your information in any way suspect? If so, reestablish the "facts" involved. Does your new information lead to any different interpretations?

21−2−2. What information have you that negates any of these interpretations?

21−2−3. Do you have too much information and too little organization?

21−2−4. Have your "facts" been corroborated by additional sources or means?

21−2−5. How accurately have you determined the symptoms of this problem?

21−2−6. How accurately is it possible to determine the symptoms of this problem?

21−2−7. How do you know your facts are correct?

21−2−8. What is there that you don't know or are unsure of?

21−2−9. Who could give you another viewpoint on this situation?

21−2−10. Can you ask someone else what they think the answer is?

21−3. Are all your facts and interpretations right?

21−3−1. What does your interpretation of the situation imply or lead to?

Are these implications supported by any facts? Do they lead to new avenues of enquiry?

21–3–2. Is there a way of leaving the facts the same but seeing them differently?

21–3–3. How many different interpretations can you think of?

21–3–4. Is there or could there be some other explanation of this?

21–3–5. Is the present explanation simplistic or trivial?—Does it restate rather than explain?

21–3–6. How might you turn any difficulties to your advantage? What new opportunities might there be? How can you exploit these?

21–3–7. Does this involve any deeper issues?

21–3–8. Is it really more complicated than this? Or more simple?

21–3–9. What psychological blockages may be involved—in yourself, or in others? What are you blind to?

21–3–10. Have you thought carefully about the extent to which cultural blockages might be at work here? What social influences might be present here? How can they be avoided?

21–4.   Can you see any decisive patterns at all?

21–4–1. What is connected to what? Can you draw a map or picture of the pieces? How is each one connected, or how could or should it be, to the others? Are there any missing connections?

21–4–2. Are there any interesting coincidences?

21–4–3. Is this the best way of grouping these relationships and elements? How else could it be done?

21–4–4. What makes you think that you have the right view of the relationships involved?

21–4–5. Can you find some minor irregularity, some small inconsistency, where things seem to be otherwise basically OK? What does this mean? Perhaps you have it all wrong after all?

21–4–6. Where is all the pressure coming from and why?

21–4–7. Is there a principal focus of complexity?

21–4–8. Which part of your problem is most disruptive, and why?

21–4–9. Which part of the problem area contributes the most positive energy, and why?

21–5. Have you checked it, even though it might seem to be "obvious?"

21–5–1. What puzzles you?

21–5–2. What contradictions or inconsistencies can you see?

21–5–3. What have you missed?

21–5–4. Is there any way of clarifying or making more specific the data which are available?

21–5–5. Is any part of the situation or solution in conflict with, or likely to be in conflict with, any other part?

21–5–6. How do the parts relate to one another? Have you established the connections?

21–5–7. When do parts get out of step?

21–5–8. Can you find a paradox in this situation?

21–5–9. Do all these elements or parts form a coherent structure—that is, do all the interrelationships, or apparent interrelationships, make sense? And does the whole thing make sense?

21–5–10. Do you have all this back to front?

21–6. As a result of the objectives, where might effort best be directed?

21–6–1. What areas are there?

21–6–2. Do they all have to be covered at this point?

21–6–3. Can they be covered? If not, which merit the most effort at this point, or which arrangement of fragments is most appropriate?

21–6–4. Which areas need the most effort, the most time, the most watching, the most thought?

21–6–5. Which activities have important sequencing or timing constraints?

21–6–6. Which activities are the most flexible, the easiest to accommodate?

21–6–7. Which activities are most subject to uncertainty?

21–6–8. Which activities will have the greatest impact if they are delayed, fail, or succeed?

21–6–9. Is it primarily a matter of getting organized, of establishing priorities, of seeing where everything fits?

21–6–10. Is it a question of discovering information, assessing the truth of something, testing, or diagnosing?

21−6−11. Is it a question of sorting out a muddled, distressing situation, avoiding some bad possibilities, or getting out of a bad situation?

21−6−12. Is it necessary to invent something new, to produce a new scheme or idea?

21−7. Can you list the decisions to be made in various circumstances?

21−7−1. Can you assign a degree of risk or uncertainty to the choice points?

21−7−2. Can you list the different strategies or approaches which can be made?

21−7−3. Can you associate with each strategy or approach the choice points, decisions, risks, and uncertainties involved?

21−7−4. Can you lay out a hierarchical structure or breakdown of sub-problems, sub-components, or decisions to be made?

21−7−5. Can you lay out a hierarchical structure or breakdown of possible choices and outcomes?

21−7−6. How many different kinds of solution to this problem might there be?

21−7−7. How many different principles and processes seem to be involved?

21−7−8. What type of solution are you looking for here, for example:

  a. An operational plan of some duration?
  b. An invention or new idea?
  c. A decision-making system or organizational structure?
  d. A conceptual structure or theory?
  e. A project plan?
  f. A search for specific information?
  g. Or what?

22. REARRANGE TO PROVOKE IDEAS (IG,SA)

22−1. Try grouping the parts of your problem according to their importance or relevance. What does this tell you?

22−1−1. Produce a checklist of specific characteristics required for your solution. Weight these for importance, cost, potential, and so on. Where does this point you?

22−1−2. Split the problem into its main aspects or dimensions, and list the elements of each aspect or dimension. Then try looking at the actual, potential, possible, and remotely conceivable interactions of all these elements with each other, one by one. What do you find that you did not expect?

22−1−3. List all the attributes or functions of each component of your problem. Consider each attribute singly for its possible contribution. Change attributes to see what the effects might be.

22−2.   Change the size of one element of the problem

22−2−1. Change the shape of one element of the problem.

22−2−2. Change the color of one element of the problem.

22−2−3. Change the weight of one element of the problem.

22−2−4. Change the value of one element of the problem.

22−2−5. Change around who does what.

22−2−6. Mix together different people in doing this.

22−2−7. Change the type of people involved.

22−2−8. Increase the number of people involved.

22−2−9. Decrease the number of people involved.

22−3.   Change the function of one element in the situation

22−3−1. Change the way in which one part of this situation is being done.

22−3−2. Change the configuration of parts or events.

22−3−3. Change the speed at which one part of the situation is happening.

22−3−4. Eliminate one of the things that are happening.

22−3−5. Add one more event or aspect to what is happening.

22−3−6. Change around the location of the parts or events.

22−3−7. What else could be constructed from this?

22−3−8. What would happen if the problem situation doubled itself, stopped, reversed, or increased tenfold?

22−3−9. Change the style of the whole operation.

22−4. Lengthen the interval between events

22−4−1. Increase the frequency of the events.

22−4−2. Decrease the frequency of events.

22−4−3. Shorten the interval between events.

22−4−4. Create more locations for these events.

22−4−5. Have fewer locations for these events.

22−4−6. Change the location of the events.

22−4−7. Lengthen the duration of events.

22−4−8. Shorten the duration of the events.

22−5. Change the number of information channels

22−5−1. Change the sequence of information flow.

22−5−2. Change the location of information exchange.

22−5−3. Change the way the information flows.

22−5−4. Change the way information is given out.

22−5−5. Change who receives information.

22−5−6. Change the way decisions are made.

22−5−7. Change the duration of decision making.

22−5−8. Change who makes the decisions.

22−5−9. Change the frequency of decision making.

22−5−10. Change the location of the decision making.

23. TAKE A DIFFERENT APPROACH (IG,SA)

23−1. How can you change your approach to this problem?

23−1−1. Is there a different way of describing your objectives? Perhaps a different statement, a different angle, or viewpoint will lead to different ideas for solutions?

23−1−2. Who could give you another viewpoint on this situation?

23−1−3. Who else could do this?

23−1−4. How many different interpretations can you think of?

23–1–5. Are you really in an environment or situation which is conducive to your own personal ability to generate new ideas? If not, why not? If you don't know what helps you can you try to find out?

23–1–6. If you had an entirely different occupation, how might this problem look to you?

23–1–7. What difference does it make to view this problem from the inside instead of from the outside, or vice versa?

23–1–8. If you pick a different area of concern—physics, technology, politics, human rights, ecology, farming, world hunger, personality, the arts, foreign trade, and so on—and try to think of your problem in those terms, what new thoughts might this offer?

23–1–9. How can you sneak up on this problem? What indirect approach can you take? What unexpected angles could you try?

23–2.   What is the most prominent, captivating, stimulating or useful-seeming aspect of this? Can you use it to find a new perspective?

23–2–1. In what direction are your ideas about this situation heading? What are you trying to achieve?—What are you trying to synthesize?—What are you trying to resolve? Can you find a different direction for this?

23–2–2. Can you change the viewpoint from which the problem is perceived, e.g.: emotional, rational, personal, organizational, political, ethical, theoretical, technical, financial, psychological, medical, etc.?

23–2–3. Would any of the above viewpoints change your perception of the problem—making it more simple, complex, understandable, or challenging?

23–2–4. Can you generate a large variety of inputs or other opinions and approaches?

23–2–5. Can you combine some hitherto separate parts of your problem?

23–2–6. Can you combine purposes? Can it do more than one thing?

23–2–7. Can you take out some of the detail, solve the simpler problem, put the detail back, and see if the solution still works?

23–2–8. Can you change the level at which you are looking at this? For example, if you have to invent a new agricultural tractor would it help to think instead of new types of cultivation, or, alternatively, of new types of motive power or drive systems? Can you take a wider view, and more specific views?

23−2−9. How can you modify the boundaries of this problem? Make it extend further, or not so far?

23−2−10. Can you focus on a weakness in your situation and turn it into an unexpected bonus?

23−2−11. Can you clear away confusing, irrelevant debris? Can the situation easily be made less fuzzy?

23−3. Why can't you change the overall system of which this is a part?

23−3−1. Why is this different from some similar operation?

23−3−2. What different larger system could this become a part of?

23−3−3. How could the objectives be changed and yet achieve the same end?

23−3−4. How can this be made different from a similar operation?

23−3−5. Change the purpose of the system which contains your problem.

23−3−6. Reorganize around the problem. Avoid the problem. Isolate the problem.

23−3−7. How are attitudes involved?

23−3−8. Can you work backwards from the effects this operation has on other areas?

23−3−9. What does it look like backwards? Can you turn the situation upside down?

23−3−10. What would happen if the problem situation doubled itself, stopped, reversed, or increased tenfold?

24. LOOK FOR SIMILAR SITUATIONS (IG)

24−1. What could be borrowed from somewhere else?

24−1−1. What other process is similar to this?

24−1−2. What else has a configuration like this?

24−1−3. Who else does something like this?

24−1−4. What else functions like this?

24−1−5. Why is this like some similar operation?

24−1−6. Is some part of this process similar to any other process?

24−1−7. Are similarities and differences trivial or crucial?

24−1−8. What makes this problem unique—anything or nothing?

24−1−9. What makes this situation unique—anything or nothing?

24−2. What analogies or metaphors for this situation can you find?

24−2−1. Can you think of any analogies from plant life, insect life, your garden or local park, the seashore, the zoo, the woods, the desert?

24−2−2. Can you find anything to spark ideas in, for example, your kitchen drawers, office drawers, a department store, your toolbox, a supermarket?

24−2−3. Are there any useful analogies to be found in electrical systems, mechanical systems, physiological systems, acoustical systems, weather systems, and so on?

24−2−4. Can you find anything comparable in history, in different social groups, cultures, civilizations?

24−2−5. What similar problems have you come across?

24−2−6. How are any similar problems similar, and how are they different?

24−2−7. How does this problem compare with and relate to other problems and events?

24−2−8. Have you come across similar situations in entirely different areas of your experience?

25. JUGGLE, JUXTAPOSE, AND FANTASIZE (IG)

25−1. Magnify the effect or characteristics of one part of your problem

25−1−1. Magnify the personal aspects.

25−1−2. Change the impact of the information flow, or communications.

25−1−3. Change the impact of decisions made.

25−1−4. Alter the kinds of information obtained, available, or sought about each element.

25−1−5. Can you pull your situation to pieces like a jigsaw puzzle and then put it back together in various different ways?

25−1−6. How can the different parts interact differently?

25−1−7. How could relationships be changed so that different events could be grouped together, or be seen to be similar? What does this tell you?

25-1-8. Think of other relationships that could exist between the parts.

25-1-9. Can you think of any way at all (think really hard) in which ideas for this situation could be sparked off by thinking about a button? A candle? A hinge? A wheel? A can? A bush? A meteor? A caterpillar? A gate? The sun? An explosion? A river? Select one or two.

25-2.   At what different period in time would this problem be significantly different? What might this tell you?

25-2-1. If the past had been different how might the situation be different?

25-2-2. Change the sequence of events.

25-2-3. Change the cause of these events.

25-2-4. Change the environment in which this is happening—to social, scientific, technological, psycological, ecological. What would the significant differences be? What does this tell you?

25-2-5. Make a different pattern with the events.

25-2-6. What special characteristics does this operation or situation have? What needs to be done to accommodate or take advantage of these?

25-2-7. Make one part of your problem larger, and another smaller.

25-3.   How could you solve this problem in a fantasy world? Why might this solution be made to work in the real world?

25-3-1. If this took place on another planet would the problem be significantly different?

25-3-2. If you were a frog, how would you perceive this problem? How would it be different? Why?

25-3-3. If this were being run by insects, how would it be organized?

25-3-4. If one of the people involved in this were a porpoise, how would things have to change?

25-3-5. Look out your window. Think how the very first thing you see could be made to relate to the problem.

25-3-6. Pretend you are one of the elements in this problem—how would you feel about it?

25−3−7. If you had a magic wand and could change this situation, how would you do it, and what does this tell you?

25−3−8. Can you see the humorous side of this? How could you make a joke using parts of this problem? How could you use that?

25−3−9. What is the most ridiculous solution you can think of? If you were put in charge of making this solution work sensibly, how would you do it? What is the craziest thing you could do? The craziest thing that could happen?

26. SYNTHESIZE (IG,SB)

26−1. **What are you trying to feel your way toward?**

26−1−1. What are you trying to grasp? What do your hunches tell you?

26−1−2. What are you trying to construct?

26−1−3. What are the bits and pieces you think are relevant?

26−1−4. What seems to be the key characteristics of this situation? What are the critical points? What is the crux of the matter?

26−11−5. What seems to be the most fruitful or rewarding direction for this to move in? In what areas are ideas or explanations for this most likely to be found?

26−1−6. How do you think these things might fit together? Have you a provisional, preliminary feeling for how this goes together?

26−1−7. What could explain this situation? Is your explanation testable or falsifiable? If not can you find one that is?

26−2. **Can you see any decisive patterns at all?**

26−2−1. Can a main focus of difficulty be isolated?

26−2−2. Is there anything, any relationship, value, structural framework, or pattern, that remains the same over any significant period of time?

26−2−3. Do you have, or can you think of, a metaphor or analogy which will help you organize all this?

26−2−4. How can you pull all this together? What means can you use to grasp it all clearly?

26−2−5. Is there some way of achieving a simpler overview of this whole thing?

26−2−6. Is there some unifying principle you can invent or borrow?

26−2−7. Is this most likely to be synthesized, developed, or explained by using pictorial or verbal methods, graphic or simulation methods, mathematical or other methods?

26−2−8. Is it too soon to attempt such a synthesis?

26−3. **What concept will synthesize all this—some old idea, or must it be something new?**

26−3−1. Do you have to try a higher level of abstraction or generality, or some other level of interpretation?

26−3−2. Is there some way you can make all this seem more concrete, easier to handle?

26−3−3. Can you deal with any structures better by thinking of them in terms of processes? For example, the structure of the human skeleton makes more sense when you look at its activities.

26−3−4. Can you deal with any processes better by thinking of how the processes evolve and develop? For example, walking can be viewed with benefit as a stage in the evolution of locomotion.

26−3−5. Is some kind of intermediate stage or idea feasible or advisable?

26−3−6. What kind of idea is required? A means of organization, a new concept, a telling metaphor, or what?

26−3−7. Can you chop it all up into broad groupings and then deal with the groupings separately, so as not to be overwhelmed by the details?

26−3−8. Are you using any idea, concept, viewpoint, metaphor, or synthesis in the most effective way?

26−3−9. Is the use of any analogy which you may be using obscuring some significant difference between the two situations?

26−3−10. Can you retain the explanatory, synthesizing power of your idea, analogy, metaphor, or viewpoint without pushing it beyond what makes sense?

26−3−11. Is the appeal of any metaphor or analogy which you are using misleading? Is it trivial?

26−4. **What will the idea, concept, theory, or model make possible? How will it do it?**

26−4−1. What will it do, explain, or make possible in a way different from the present one?

26−4−2. What will it do, explain, or make possible in the same way as now?

26−4−3. What will it fail to do, explain, or make possible, that is already happening?

26−4−4. What will it do, explain, or make possible, that is not yet happening?

26−4−5. What experimental work or further work will it generate?

26−4−6. What would it take to refute it, disprove it, or otherwise knock it down?

26−4−7. How general is it?—How widely applicable?

26−4−8. How can it be made more simple, more powerful, more effective, more significant, more wide-ranging in its application?

26−4−9. Does this synthesis, viewpoint, or metaphor just lead to explanations of the current situation, or does it predict, generate new hypotheses, produce fruitful new avenues for exploration?

27. DEVELOP IDEAS INTO SOLUTIONS (SB)

27−1. How many different kinds of solution to this problem might there be?

27−1−1. How many different principles and processes seem to be involved?

27−1−2. What type of solution are you looking for here, e.g.:

    a. An operational plan of some duration?

    b. An invention or new idea?

    c. A decision-making system or organizational structure?

    d. A conceptual structure or theory?

    e. A project plan?

    f. A search for specific information?

    g. Or what?

27−1−3. Do you have clear exactly what it is you are trying to achieve? What general state of affairs are you trying to bring about?

27−1−4. What has to be balanced against what else? What pieces have to be made to interlock?

27−1−5. Which parts could assist or support each other if acting together? Can this be arranged?

27−1−6. Which parts would weaken the solution if placed together? Can this be avoided?

27−1−7. What new elements, possibilities, opportunities does your idea provide? How, where, when, why, for whom?

27−1−8. Against what political, organizational, policy, or ideological background will your solution be built? How will your solution fit into it?

27−1−9. Who will resent or resist your solution, and why? What can be done about it?

27−1−10. Is there anything bothering you about this solution? Are you facing it or covering it up?

27−2. As a result of the objectives, where might effort best be directed?

27−2−1. What areas are there?

27−2−2. Do they all have to be covered at this point?

27−2−3. Can they all be covered? If not, which merit the most effort at this point, and which arrangement of fragments is most appropriate?

27−2−4. Which areas need the most effort, the most time, the most watching, the most thought?

27−2−5. Which activities have important sequencing or timing constraints? What is the best sequencing and timing of these?

27−2−6. Which activities are the most flexible, the easiest to accommodate?

27−2−7. Which activities are the most subject to uncertainty?

27−2−8. Which activities will have the greatest impact if they are delayed, fail, or succeed?

27−2−9. Who can help you with this?

27−3. What are the major variables and decision sequences?

27−3−1. What will be the component parts of your new situation? Have you specified these?

27−3−2. What are your targets?—What time is required?—What are your deadlines and priorities?

27−3−3. What are your alternate plans and priorities?—What are your emergency plans?

27−3−4. Do all these elements or parts form a coherent structure? Do all their interrelationships, or apparent interrelationships, make sense?

27−3−5. What relationship does each element have with each other element?

27−3−6. How does each old problem element relate to the new situation?

27−3−7. How many distinct sub-sections or sub-systems should the solution have?

27−3−8. How many levels of organization should the solution have? How will it be tied together?

27−3−9. If there is any uncertainty in the solution, have you located it clearly?

27−3−10. Have you been specific about how you will deal with any uncertainty?

27−3−11. To what extent is it possible to make a formal (mathematical, logical, or quantitative) statement of the relationships between variables or parts of the problem?

27−4. **In what directions can you best develop your idea?**

27−4−1. Can you develop it by following up on all the ramifications and implications?

27−4−2. Would it help to look for further ideas, information, or analogies?

27−4−3. Do any other things need to happen to make your solution possible? If so, how are you going to ensure that they do?

27−4−4. Have you considered ramifications outside the immediate problem area?

27−4−5. What will happen in other areas when you initiate activity in the areas you are working on? Establish the implications and ramifications.

27−4−6. How much support does this system require in terms of people's time, materials, equipment, energy, coordination, etc.?

27−4−7. How should this be arranged or organized?

27−4−8. What decision-making structure is required?

27−4−9. What information structure is required?

28.   DEVISE INFORMATION AND DECISION-MAKING ROUTES (SB)

28−1.   What organization is decision-making and information flow to support?

28−1−1.   How will decision-making and information flow act to support a coherent overall organization?

28−1−2.   How will decision making and information act as a reliable, effective, and adaptable link between planning or directing and the resultant actions?

28−1−3.   How will decision making and information tie together the various functions involved?

28−1−4.   What decision modes are required in this command, control, or organizational arrangement?

28−1−5.   What information channels will connect the organized functions with those responsible for directing the system toward its objectives?

28−1−6.   How flexible does the organizational structure have to be?

28−1−7.   How will the appropriate flexibility be introduced into the decision-making network?

28−1−8.   How will it be possible to make information flow fast and flexible enough to permit future-directed planning?

28−2.   What decision-making structure is required?

28−2−1.   Who will make decisions?

28−2−2.   How will decisions be made?

28−2−3.   What is needed to make the decisions?

28−2−4.   Who will be involved in the decision-making chain?

28−2−5.   What information will result from decision-making processes?

28−2−6.   How will the decision-making structure work? With what impact are decisions made?

28−2−7.   How quickly can decisions be made?

28−2−8.   Will information be available when needed?

28−3.   What information structure is required?

28−3−1. How must information be arranged, organized, sequenced?

28−3−2. Who needs to know what?

28−3−3. What information is required to look ahead?

28−3−4. What information will cause or trigger decision making?

28−3−5. How fast should information be available?

28−3−6. How much information is too much?—Too little? How much redundancy is required, appropriate, or permissible?

28−3−7. When should information be available?

28−3−8. What routes should information take?

**28−4.   What is the content of each message in terms of information, form,
and function?**

28−4−1. What are the components of this message?

28−4−2. How does the message fit into the decision-making or operating
structure?

28−4−3. To whom is this message addressed?

28−4−4. Is this message primarily for decision making, for learning, for
speculatory purposes?—Or is it multi-purpose?

28−4−5. In what manner or format should information best be transmitted
or received?

28−4−6. How should information best travel—via what medium?

28−4−7. Will information best be transmitted as sight, sound, words,
pictures, or combinations?—Or by feel, touch, and so on?

28−4−8. Is maximum effect important?—Or maximum speed, maximum
retention, or what?

29.   BUILD MODEL OF THE SITUATION (D,SB)

**29−1.   Do you have clear exactly what it is you are trying to achieve? What
general state of affairs are you trying to bring about?**

29−1−1. Can you lay out a hierarchical structure or breakdown of sub-
problems, sub-components, or decisions to be made?

29-1-2. Can you lay out a hierarchical structure or breakdown of possible choices and outcomes?

29-1-3. Can you list the decisions to be made in various circumstances?

29-1-4. Can you assign a degree of risk or uncertainty to the choice points?

29-1-5. Can you list the different strategies or approaches which can be made?

29-1-6. Can you associate with each strategy or approach the choice points, decisions, risks, and uncertainties involved?

29-2.   Can you build a working model of your situation?—physical, conceptual or mathematical?—a sketch, flowchart, or idea structure?

29-2-1. How broad or how limited is the context which this model must represent or fit into?

29-2-2. What specific objectives is this model trying to satisfy?

29-2-3. Can you quantify or measure your situation's components in such a way that a testable model can be built?

29-2-4. To what extent is it possible to make a formal—mathematical, logical, quantitative—statement of the relationships between variables or parts of the problem?

29-2-5. If the situation is not amenable to quantification, are you going to waste time attempting it?

29-2-6. What kind of modelling, simulating, gaming, or representational process is most appropriate to this situation? Does it accord with the real world level of complexity or abstraction?

29-2-7. How close can your model come to real life without being too cumbersome or complicated to operate quickly and simply?

29-2-8. If your model cannot be made detailed or complex enough to represent real life sufficiently, are you using the wrong approach, or the wrong kind of modelling?

29-3.   Can you build up a structure, pattern, or model of the events which arranges the observed data in a way that matches the real world or the predicted real world?

29-3-1. What are the major variables and decision sequences?

29-3-2. How many distinct sub-sections or sub-systems should the solution have?

29−3−3. How many levels of organization should the solution have? How will it all be tied together?

29−3−4. What can you do with the model? How much can you achieve with it? Is it trivial?

29−3−5. How can you improve the model? Could corresponding improvements be made in the real world?

29−3−6. Can the model be modified easily? Does it change as fast as the real world?

29−3−7. Is this the kind of situation in which subtracting or changing just one element, or adding just one more, will change the character of the situation radically?

29−3−8. If the problem's solution is insensitive to a particular variable, or if the variable or part is trivial or irrelevant, can you keep it out of your model and your solution building and assessment?

29−3−9. Have you left out any aspect of the problem unintentionally?

29−4. Does your model permit you to operate it over and over, and get a clear picture of how it might operate in the real world?

29−4−1. Does your model make fundamental relationships explicit, or do they remain vague or fuzzy?

29−4−2. If there is uncertainty in the situation, is it completely uncertain and completely unpredictable, or is it uncertain within particular limits, and can some kind of probability be assigned to the situation?

29−4−3. Are you allowing the quantified and predictable structure of your model to overshadow any basic uncertainty or variability in the situation it is modelling?

29−4−4. How will you test it?

29−4−5. Do you have data to test your model?

29−4−6. How far can you test your model before putting it into effect as a solution? Be ingenious.

29−4−7. Can you test your model mathematically, as a game, by simulation, by linear programming, by field tests, logically, or mechanically? In how many ways and how effectively or reliably?

29−4−8. When principal aspects, values, or parameters of the model are changed, do the results change in a consistent and plausible way? In other words, does the model seem to be realistic, and does it make good, testable predictions?

30.   INITIAL ASSESSMENT OF SOLUTION (SA)

30−1.   Is this doomed from the start?

30−1−1. Are you sure this is what you really want or what is really needed?

30−1−2. Are you hoping this will work out, even though it would require good luck rather than good management?

30−1−3. Are you closing your eyes to anything?

30−1−4. Where are the greatest risks? Where are the greatest challenges? Can these be handled?

30−1−5. Has this been thought through thoroughly?

30−1−6. Does it form a coherent whole? Does it hang together properly?

30−1−7. What is there that you don't know or are unsure of?

30−1−8. Are there any loose ends? If so, why?

30−1−9. What have you missed?

30−1−10. Do you have it all back to front?

30−2.   Don't you really need a broader outlook? Are you looking at the situation from too limited a perspective?

30−2−1. Are you carrying an inappropriate set of expectations into this situation—concerning results, your own behavior, the behavior of others, the future, capacities, possibilities?

30−2−2. Should you draw in your horns and look at a smaller range of events?

30−2−3. Should a larger, encompassing problem be attacked?

30−2−4. Is any part of the situation or solution in conflict with, or likely to be in conflict with, any other part?

30−2−5. How do the parts relate to one another? Have you established the connections?

30−2−6. When do parts get out of step?

30−2−7. Can you find a paradox in this situation?

30−2−8. Do all these elements or parts form a coherent structure? Do all the interrelationships, or apparent interrelationships, make sense?

30−2−9. What puzzles you?

30−2−10. What contradictions or inconsistencies can you see?

30−3. Is it really more complicated than this, or more simple?

30−3−1. Does this involve any deeper issues?

30−3−2. Are you looking at more than one solution seriously—or have you rushed for the one which seems to solve the most immediate aspects of the problem?

30−3−3. Have you checked it, even though it might seem obvious?

30−3−4. Are the objectives of different parts of the solution, or the system into which the solution will fit, consistent? Do any objectives conflict with each other?

30−3−5. Has this been thoroughly researched?

30−3−6. If the solution's claim is to novelty, has it been done before anyway?

30−3−7. If the solution's claim is comprehensiveness, has it perhaps omitted something?

30−3−8. Do you have the most up-to-date picture?

30−3−9. Are you using the most up-to-date, sophisticated, advanced model or approach to your problem? If not, could you use it? How could you find out? How could you learn to use it?

30−3−10. Are you afraid to throw it all out and start again?

30−3−11. Is this problem solving or: panic, self-justification, avoidance, rationalization, or . . . ?

30−4. What is the scope of this idea?

30−4−1. In what areas will it be expected to resolve problems, offer insights, or in general be productive?

30−4−2. What do you have to do to test whether your idea does in fact contribute to these areas?

30−4−3. From what areas do you expect the main support of your idea to be drawn? Where might you expect peripheral support?

30−4−4. What other ideas are there, or have there been, that in any way resemble your idea, or were set up to deal with your concerns?

30−4−5. How does your idea match these other ideas?

30−4−6. What other ideas are there, or have there been, which draw the opposite or very different conclusions from your idea?

30−4−7. What do you make of that?

30−4−8. In what places have others gone further than you? How? Why?

30−4−9. Has your idea solved the problem, shifted it, or disguised it?

31. DETERMINE IMPLICATIONS AND RAMIFICATIONS (SB,SA)

31−1. Where does this problem fit in the general scheme of things?

31−1−1. How does this problem compare and relate to other problems and events?

31−1−2. Is this part of a larger system or problem, and closely related to it?

31−1−3. What is connected to what? Can you draw a map or picture of the pieces? How is each one connected, or how could or should it be, to others? Are there any missing connections?

31−1−4. How many different principles and processes seem to be involved?

31−1−5. What are the most important parts, relationships, or outcomes?

31−1−6. What are the priorities?

31−1−7. Do all these elements or parts form a coherent structure? Do all their interrelationships, or apparent interrelationships, make sense, and does the whole thing make sense?

31−2. What relationship does each element have with each other element?

31−2−1. What else is connected to this, either directly or indirectly?

31−2−2. What is the nature or manner of these connections?

31−2−3. What can be inferred from this? What is implied by this?

31−2−4. How closely connected to this situation are these other events, principles, functions, concepts?

31−2−5. Are any connections permanent or stable?—Or intermittent, chancy, arbitrary or irregular?

31—2—6. What events include or form a necessary part of other events?

31—2—7. Are connections one-way, two-way, or variable?

31—2—8. Is there a hierarchy of connections, or do all events exert similar influence?

31—3.   Is this going to affect something else?

31—3—1. To what degree is this linked to, approaching, or on a collision course with anything else?

31—3—2. How can it be affected by anything else linked to it?

31—3—3. How can it affect anything else linked to it?

31—3—4. When and why might this occur?

31—3—5. How and with what results?

31—3—6. What would be done in such an eventuality?

31—4.   Have you analysed the various solutions proposed with respect to any trade-offs that may have to be made?

31—4—1. If each of your solutions has a number of possible outcomes, and you cannot decide which solution is best, can you decide which solution contains an outcome which would be worst?

31—4—2. To what extent are resources used up, costs incurred, or danger courted, if each alternative solution satisifies the objectives involved?

31—4—3. Who grows, develops, or benefits as a result of this situation?

31—4—4. Who suffers as a result of this situation?

31—4—5. What duration, cost, urgency, potential, and priority are associated with each component or relationship?

31—4—6. Why is the framework that contains the problem structured the way it is? Can this be changed? Will it change anyway? What will happen if it does?

31—4—7. What does your interpretation of the situation imply or lead to? Are these implications supported by any facts? Do they lead to new avenues of enquiry?

31—4—8. Have you considered ramifications outside the immediate problem area?

31−4−9. If the problem is organizational, have you considered emotional factors too? If it is a people problem, have you remembered costs?

32. ATTEMPT IMPROVEMENT (SB,SA)

32−1. How can this be made more effective?—more powerful?—more significant?

32−1−1. How can this be made more appealing? How can this be made more persuasive?

32−1−2. How can this be made more simple? Is there a simpler answer than this?

32−1−3. How can this be made quicker?

32−1−4. How can this be made more compact?

32−1−5. How can this be made more flexible?

32−1−6. How can this be made more stimulating? How can this be made more motivating?

32−1−7. If you have a model, how can you improve·the model? Could corresponding improvements be made in the real world?

32−1−8. How can this be made to work with less energy, attention, or maintenance?

32−1−9. How can this be made to do more with the same input?

32−1−10. How can this be made more useful?

32−2. Could you improve your solution by extending it to work in other situations?

32−2−1. Can it cover a broader spectrum of events? What would be required to make this possible?

32−2−2. Can you pursue this in greater depth, with greater energy, or with greater talent?

32−2−3. Does your solution apply to anything other than the immediate situation? Can you extend its principles to other areas?

32−2−4. Could it be blended with some other idea to produce something new?

32−2−5. What is the best part? Can it be made better?

32−2−6. What is the worst part? Can it be eliminated?

32−2−7. What have you missed? What have you forgotten?

32−2−8. Are you making any mistakes or misinterpretations?

32−2−9. How might you turn any difficulties to your advantage? What new opportunities might there be? How can you exploit these?

32−3. Can you change your approach to this problem?

32−3−1. Now that you have found the obvious solution can you find one which is less obvious?

32−3−2. How could you get a fresh look at this?

32−3−3. Is there a more bold or adventurous way of doing this?

32−3−4. Are you afraid to throw it all out and start again?

32−3−5. Is this too cumbersome, too involved, too tedious?

32−3−6. Are you being complacent or being misled?

32−3−7. Could you have a better attitude to this? Could you be more positive, more optimistic?

32−3−8. Can you focus on a weakness in your situation and turn it into an unexpected bonus?

33. PREPARE IMPLEMENTATION PLANS (SB)

33−1. How do you plan to transfer your solution from your head—or from paper—to real life?

33−1−1. What style of operating, approach, or behavior is most appropriate?

33−1−2. What kind of approach most suits the kind of uncertainty or complexity in this situation?

33−1−3. What priority for implementation should this have?

33−1−4. Should it be phased in gradually?

33−1−5. Is an interim solution demanded while a more thorough investigation is undertaken?

33−1−6. How are future developments likely to affect this system?

33−1−7. Is a pilot scheme or some kind of trial run called for?

33−1−8. Can this new scheme be operated in parallel with the old situation for comparative purposes, or for phase-in?

33−1−9. How else could you get a feel for what might happen—without jeopardizing anything?

33−2. As a result of the objectives, where might effort be best directed?

33−2−1. What areas are there?

33−2−2. Do they all have to be covered at this point?

33−2−3. Can they be covered? If not, which merit the most effort at this point, or which arrangement of fragments is most appropriate?

33−2−4. Which areas need the most effort, the most time, the most watching, the most thought?

33−2−5. Which activities have important sequencing or timing constraints? Which is the best sequencing and timing of these?

33−2−6. Which activities are the most subject to uncertainty?

33−2−7. Which activities are the most flexible, the easiest to accommodate?

33−2−8. Which activities will have the greatest impact if they are delayed, fail, or succeed?

33−2−9. Do any other things need to happen to make your solution possible? If so, how are you going to make sure they do?

33−2−10. What will happen in other areas when you initiate activity in the areas you are working on? Establish the implications and ramifications.

33−2−11. Who can help you with this?

33−3. Is implementation properly planned and organized?

33−3−1. What steps and stages are required? What will you do if these get out of joint?

33−3−2. What steps will you take to make sure the separate parts of the project interlink smoothly?

33−3−3. How will you time the implementation of your solution? When would be a good time? When would be a bad time?

33−3−4. How long will implementation take? Who will be involved? Can they do it?

33-3-5. Has a program been developed for assessing the solution's success?

33-3-6. Is everyone fully aware of the implementation plan and its implications?

33-3-7. Is the solution fully understood by everyone involved?

33-3-8. If permission or authority is required, has this been obtained?

33-3-9. If funding is required, is it already instituted or available?

33-3-10. Is everyone aware of who is accountable for what?

33-3-11. Are all changes understood and accepted by those affected?

33-3-12. Who will resent or resist this solution, and why? What can be done about it?

33-4. What progress checkpoints will there be?

33-4-1. How will you watch out for side effects or unanticipated future problems?

33-4-2. What will you do if things don't go according to plan?

33-4-3. In the event of being able to accomplish only some of your objectives, what are your priorities?

33-4-4. If it is not possible to think of a better solution and there are still areas uncontrolled, can you develop plans to deal with possible difficulties?

33-4-5. If you can see anything that might go wrong, do you have a contingency plan for it?

33-4-6. Are the contingency plans likely to work?

33-4-7. What would happen if your solution failed completely? Have you a plan for that?

33-4-8. Have you planned for the solution's demise—either soon and unexpectedly, or later and anticipatedly?

33-4-9. Imagine a disaster for your solution. How would you avoid it?

33-4-10. What will you do in case of emergency? How will you organize yourself?—What will you have ready to put into action?

33-4-11. How might you make up for lost time or lost progress, if this is required?

34.   PROJECT THE SOLUTION INTO THE FUTURE (SB,SA)

34—1.   Will this idea work in the future?

34—1—1.   How are future developments likely to affect this system?

34—1—2.   Who will resent or resist this solution, and why? What can be done about it?

34—1—3.   If you take each element of the solution and extend it into the future, will the arrangements of components still be the same? If not, will your solution still work?

34—1—4.   Can you figure out what will replace the present situation and its solution?

34—1—5.   Will your solution harmonize with future developments, and with its replacement?

34—1—6.   If you can see anything that might go wrong, do you have a contingency plan for it?

34—1—7.   Have you planned for the possibility of the solution's demise, either soon and unexpectedly, or later and unanticipatedly?

34—1—8.   Can you imagine a disaster for your solution? How would you avoid such a disaster?

34—1—9.   What if some unexpectedly beneficial future event occurs? Is there enough flexibility in your solution to permit you to gain maximum advantage from this?

34—1—10.   What would happen if the problem situation doubled itself, stopped, reversed, or increased tenfold?

34—2.   How will demand for this system grow or change in the future? Why?

34—2—1.   How will demand by this system for resources grow or change in the future? Why?

34—2—2.   What are the growing edges of the situation for which the solution is, or is to be, designed? How many are there, and how do they interact? How interdependent are their growth rates? How vigorous is their growth? Which ones will present the most serious problems to your solution? How will your solution cope with them?

34−2−3. Is there some reason why the future in this situation may differ considerably from the past?

34−2−4. What would happen if your solution failed completely? Have you a plan for that?

34−2−5. Can you imagine several different futures? Can your solution handle all these? What if something entirely different happens?

34−2−6. Can you think of any reasons why your solution might make things worse?

34−2−7. Could your solution last twice as long as it is intended to?

34−2−8. Are you looking far enough ahead?

34−2−9. What are your long-term aims?

34−2−10. Does this perceived or designed structure make sense if extended in time?

35.   ASSESS ENERGY AND CONTRIBUTION OF THE SOLUTION (SA)

35−1.   What and where are the strong points? How much energy does this contribute?

35−1−1. Is this inventive? Does it permit and encourage the generation of new ideas, forms, structures, or concepts? Does it promote diversity and richness?

35−1−2. Is this flexible? Does it permit and encourage quick changes of direction or shape?

35−1−3. Is this adaptive? Does it permit and encourage quick response to changing internal and external circumstances?

35−1−4. Can this handle, tolerate, generate, reduce complexity?

35−1−5. Can this produce simplicity? Reduce chaos? Provide pattern? Provide clear perceptions?

35−1−6. Can this maintain chosen levels and degrees of stability?

35−1−7. How much information can this handle, generate, or seek, and through how many different channels or media?

35−1−8. What have you done to ensure that this problem will never recur?

35−1−9. If it is not possible to think of a better solution and there are still uncontrolled areas, can you develop plans to deal with possible difficulties?

35-2. Does your solution contribute more energy to surrounding systems than previously, or is all the energy directed inward?

35-2-1. What kinds of demands does this system satisfy? How important are they?

35-2-2. Will the solution upset the energy balance of the overall system? Will it set events moving at different speeds and out of phase with each other?

35-2-3. How can you get more of a contribution, more energy, out of this solution?

35-2-4. When faced with difficulty will this system or solution maintain its organization and ability to respond, or will it become disorganized and ineffective?

35-2-5. Is this system potentially fruitful of new ideas or new developments?

35-2-6. Is everything in balance, in harmony?

35-2-7. Is this solution integrative, cooperative? Does it pull together, rather than wrench apart? Does it tend toward harmonious balance, even though this balance may fluctuate?

35-3. Does your solution allow for personal growth, and growth in general?

35-3-1. Does your solution enhance anyone's growth or fulfilment?

35-3-2. Does your solution optimize motivation?

35-3-3. What obstacles to human advancement might this solution help overcome?

35-3-4. As a result of working with this system or solution will a person be more able to deal with this kind of problem and related problems in future?

35-3-5. What will people be able to do more easily as a result of this solution? Is this valuable?

35-3-6. As a result of this design or solution, is anyone likely to have some good ideas? Is this solution stimulating?

35-4. How far ahead can disaster be predicted?

35-4-1. How long does it take for a disaster or potential disaster to be recognized as such?

35−4−2. How quickly is it possible to regroup to deal with disaster?

35−4−3. What kinds of disaster can this system recover from, and what kinds will destroy it?

35−4−4. Can this disaster be handled with minimal impact on the aims and occupations of the system?

35−4−5. Can the aims, objectives, occupations of the system quickly take on new expression during and after disaster?

35−4−6. What amount of planning, forecasting, and problem seeking goes on within this system? Is this a problem?

35−4−7. What amount of planning, forecasting, and problem seeking goes on in systems affecting your solution?

35−4−8. Who is involved in the planning, forecasting, and problem-seeking effort? Is it well done?

35−4−9. Where is the positive, integrative energy in this system located? At what points in the process does this occur, around what elements and relationships, and at what times? What is the source of the effort that holds it all together and keeps it moving?

35−4−10. Are there peaks in the integrative activity in this system? When, how, and where do they occur?

36.   ASSESS IMPACT AND WEAKNESSES OF SOLUTION (SA)

36−1. **What and where are the weak points?**

36−1−1. Does your solution have any guiding theme or principle, or is it merely stop-gap?

36−1−2. What is this situation or solution unprepared for?

36−1−3. Who is causing any detrimental planning, forecasting, or problem seeking that exists in systems affecting your situation?

36−1−4. Will significant changes be caused by this system? If so, will they be toward growth or decline?

36−1−5. Is there anything about your solution that bothers you? Will it destroy your solution? If so, it is better if this happens before implementation rather than after.

36−1−6. Does this system consume resources that could be better used elsewhere?

36−1−7. Does this consume more resources than are merited by its output and value?

36−1−8. To what extent are resources used up, costs incurred, or danger courted, as each alternative solution satisfies the objectives involved?

36−2.   Does your solution inhibit anyone's growth or fulfilment?

36−2−1. Does this fail to offer opportunity for growth, fulfilment, diversity, or richness of experience?

36−2−2. If your solution involves people, have you structured their roles or environment for them, or for yourself, in such a way that their functioning will be less than it might be?

36−2−3. Do those involved have access to appropriate information in order to make decisions?

36−2−4. Are those involved put into too many conflicts, with no intervening periods for regaining composure?

36−2−5. Is the effort really structured properly? Do those involved have too many decisions to make in a short time—thus increasing stress? Do they have too many fluctuations in work flow? Or too few?

36−2−6. Who suffers as a result of this situation?

36−2−7. How sensitive to the presence and anticipation of problems is this system?

36−2−8. Can the users of the solution modify it? Or will it be rigid and non-adaptive?

36−3.   What degree of irregularity of supply, energy, interest, pressure, or acceptance will cause this system to fail?

36−3−1. At what point will this system fail through too low a level of supply, energy, interest, pressure, or acceptance?

36−3−2. At what point will this system fail through too high a level of supply, energy, interest, pressure, or acceptance?

36−3−3. What degree of irregularity of demand will cause this system to fail?

36−3−4. At what point will this system fail through too high a level of demand, load, competition, pressure, stress, or change?

36−3−5. At what point will this system fail through too low a level of demand, load, competition, pressure, stress, or change?

36−3−6. Are there peaks in the disruptive activity in the system? When, how, and where do they occur?

37. CHECK RESULTS OF SOLUTION (SA)

37−1. Did the solution work? If not, why did it fail? How long did it survive, and why?

37−1−1. If the solution has failed, can it be patched up until a new one is ready?

37−1−2. If the solution has failed, is it too late to adjust it?

37−1−3. If the solution has failed, was it completely inadequate and out of touch with the reality of the situation?

37−1−4. If the solution has failed, has it upset anything else and if so what will you do about it?

37−1−5. Does the reason for failure present you with any insights?

37−1−6. Does your solution inhibit anyone's growth or fulfilment?

37−1−7. If your solution involves people, have you structured their roles or environment for them, or for yourself, in such a way that their functioning will be less than it might be?

37−1−8. Do those involved have access to appropriate information in order to make decisions?

37−1−9. Are those involved put into too many conflicts, with no intervening periods for regaining composure?

37−1−10. Is the effort really structured properly? Do those involved have too many decisions to make in a short time—thus increasing stress? Do they have too many fluctuations in work flow? Or too few?

37−2. If the solution was a success, can it be improved?

37−2−1. Has the solution or its effects presented any new opportunities? If so, what can be done to exploit these?

37−2−2. If the solution was a success, does this give any opportunity to tackle a problem looming on the horizon?

37−2−3. Did you have to put more into producing the solution than you expected?

37−2−4. Was the solution worth the effort? Was the effort disproportionate to the value of the solution?

37−2−5. Having solved your problem, does anything now look very different from your new viewpoint? If so, could this suggest yet another way of solving it?

37−2−6. If you look at the situation from a greater distance, in broader perspective, how does your solution measure up?

37−2−7. Is the solution fully understood by everyone involved?

37−2−8. Does your solution allow for personal growth, and for growth in general?

37−2−9. Does your solution enhance anyone's growth or fulfilment?

37−2−10. Does your solution optimize motivation?

37−3. How well did the solution or approach work?

37−3−1. Does the solution meet the requirements or objectives previously established?

37−3−2. What and where are the weak points?

37−3−3. What and where are the strong points?

37−3−4. Can you find some minor irregularity, some small inconsistency where things seem to be otherwise basically OK? What does all this mean? Do you perhaps have it all wrong after all?

37−3−5. What unforseen problems arose and why?

37−3−6. What delays and disruptions were there, and why?

37−3−7. Is the solution really working, or are appearances deceiving you?

37−3−8. Is the solution going to continue working like this, or is something going to go wrong sooner or later?

38. ASSESS MERITS AND DEFECTS OF THIS STRATEGY (AA)

38−1. How well did the approach work?

38−1−1. What and where are the strong points? What do you think the good points about your approach have been? Efficiency? Speed? Interest? Enjoyment?

38−1−2. What and where are the weak points? What do you think the bad points about your approach have been? Wrong direction? Too cumbersome? Disorganized? Uninspired?

38−1−3. Have there been any surprises? If so, why?

38−1−4. Look at the points where you didn't feel so sure of yourself. Why was this? Is it important? What can you do about it?

38−1−5. Is there anything you consistently overlook, don't pay much attention to, emphasize, or concentrate on when looking at problems? How is that affecting this situation?

38−1−6. Is there anything about your way of solving problems that generates further problems, or fails to solve problems, and guarantees their continuance?

38−1−7. Have you put in many stop-gap solutions recently? If so, why not try to view the situation from a higher, more abstract, more detached manner?

38−2. Have you made a genuine advance?

38−2−1. Were the activities undertaken adequate?

38−2−2. Were the activities undertaken related as closely as possible to the objectives?

38−2−3. Was enough done?

38−2−4. Was what was done done well enough?

38−2−5. Were the overall objectives attained?

38−2−6. Did the situation change such that:

    a. tactics needed to be changed?
    b. overall strategy needed to be changed?
    c. overall objectives needed to be changed? Why?

38−2−7. Did you minimize activities that did not contribute directly to overall objectives? Did you maximize those that did?

38−2−8. Did you get enough feedback, response, contribution?

38−2−9. Did you communicate effectively, appealingly, honestly?

38−3. Was this the most effective way of doing this? Was this the best action you could have taken?

38−3−1. Could you have done this faster? Could you have done it sooner?

38−3−2. Did you waste time anywhere?

38−3−3. Did you move at the appropriate speed?

38−3−4. Did you cover this in sufficient depth?

38−3−5. Did you make a genuine contribution?

38−3−6. Did you dissipate your efforts? Could your work have been more concentrated?

38−3−7. Was anything placed in jeopardy?

38−3−8. Was this problem solving or: panic, self-justification, avoidance, rationalization, or . . .?

38−4.   How can you benefit from this situation for similar situations in the future?

38−4−1. Look ahead. What kinds of problems might you come across in future for which your approach or way of constructing strategies would be inadequate or useless?

38−4−2. Can you think of any other ways to go about solving problems in general, and this problem in particular?

38−4−3. Can you think of any possible disadvantages of having taken this approach with this problem? With any problem?

38−4−4. Are you taking the same approach as usual in solving this one?

38−4−5. Is your strategy appropriate to the problem?

38−4−6. Have you used this strategy before? Perhaps you should now be using an improved version?

38−4−7. Are you keeping in mind the objectives for solving this problem, or is technique or a particular aspect of the problem clouding your vision?

38−4−8. If other people were involved, can you ask them the above questions?

38−5.   Having solved your problem, does anything look very different from your new viewpoint? If so, could this suggest yet another way of approaching problems?

38−5−1. Could you have perceived the situation in an entirely different way and have built a superior strategy?

38−5−2. What have you done to ensure that this problem will never recur?

38−5−3. Can you improve your problem-solving methods so that you can produce better solutions faster in the future?

38−5−4. Are there any steps in your problem solving that could be eliminated, reversed, changed, added to?

38−5−5. Have you been acting in a flexible, imaginative, adaptive, inventive, coherent manner?—Would anyone else agree with your answer? Ask them.

38−5−6. What experiences have other people had who have gone through this kind of thing? What did they learn? How can you find out?

38−5−7. Did your approach allow the appropriate skills and problem-solving techniques to be optimally deployed?

INDEX